The Book On Community-Led Strategy

How the Most Resilient Brands Grow Through Belonging, Participation, and Trust

I0095482

The Book On Series

By Sabir Chatte

Published by The Book On Publishing, 2025.

First edition. June 6, 2025.

Website: https://thebookon.ca

Substack: https://thebookonpublishing.substack.com/

While every precaution has been taken in the preparation of this book, the publisher assumes no responsibility for errors or omissions, or damages resulting from the use of the information contained herein.

THE BOOK ON COMMUNITY LED STRATEGY

First edition. June 6, 2025.
Copyright © 2025 The Book On Publishing
ISBN: 978-1-997795-84-1

Written by Sabir Chatte.

The Book On Series

The Book On Life Unscripted

The Book On Risk Management in Payments

The Book On AI for Everyday People

The Book On Relationships

The Book On Master The Algorithm

The Book On Saying No

The Book On Community Led Strategy

The Book On The Myth of Multitasking

The Book On The Burnout Blueprint

The Book On The Digital Reboot

The Book On The Shape of What's Coming

The Book On Strategic Obsession

The Book On High-Stakes Thinking

The Book On Artificial Leverage

The Book On Clarity

The Book On Uncertainty

The Book On Operational Excellence

The Book On Escape

Table of Contents

Read This First

This is not a book designed to entertain you. It's not here to charm, to soothe, or to hold your hand. It won't dazzle you with stories, metaphors, or motivational fluff. What you're having is a tool, an instruction manual written for people who are serious about learning, executing, and thinking at a higher level.

Every book in The Book On Series is built on a single premise: clarity beats complexity. We believe that when you strip away the noise, the emotions, the marketing spin, and the cultural rituals of "self-help," what's left is raw, unembellished instruction. That's what these books offer.

They are dry by design. Not because we don't care about language or narrative, but because when you're building something that matters, you don't need more distractions. You need a clear architecture. Mental scaffolding. Direction that respects your intelligence.

Each title in this series takes on a specific domain: decision-making, clarity, strategy, leverage, and uncertainty, and drills deep, not in sweeping generalizations, but in applied frameworks. These are books for builders, operators, founders, tacticians, and thinkers, people who don't just consume knowledge but operationalize it.

You'll find no chapter-long anecdotes here. No self-congratulatory memoirs. No bullet-point platitudes. Instead, what you'll get is structured insight: argument, example, application. The tone is direct. The prose is sober. The ideas are designed to be lifted out and used.

You won't be coddled, but you won't be misled either.

There's a place in the world for lyrical, emotional, story-driven books, and this isn't that place. This is a workspace. A blueprint. A conversation for people who are ready to act, not just absorb.

We respect your time and your intellect.

Welcome to The Book On Series.

Dedication

For the invisible architects,

those who build trust without titles,

create culture without credit,

and hold space long before the room has a name.

This book is yours.

- S.C.

Epigraph

"There is no power for change greater than a community discovering what it cares about."
- Margaret J. Wheatley

Acknowledgments

This book carries more names than mine.

To the community builders, strategists, organizers, and quiet stewards who generously shared their stories, thank you for teaching me what real belonging looks like, especially when no one is watching.

To the companies and collectives that let me listen from the inside and the outside, your openness shaped every page.

To The Book On Team and David Webb, your clarity, courage, and early belief meant more than you know.

And to the readers who showed up not to extract answers, but to build better questions, you are already part of what's next.

Preface

Why I Wrote This Book, and Who It's For

I didn't set out to write a book about community. I set out to understand why some companies feel alive, and others don't.

You've probably felt the difference yourself. Some businesses sell products, raise capital, and even hit growth metrics, yet they somehow feel brittle. They build audiences, but not loyalty. They generate demand, but not belief.

Then some companies feel different. They move with momentum that can't be traced back to ad spend or clever features. People talk about them with energy. They recommend them not because they're told to, but because they want to. And more importantly, they don't just buy, they build, contribute, defend, and stay.

At the center of that difference is a force we call "community."

Not in the marketing sense. Not in the warm-and-fuzzy HR sense. But in the strategic sense. As a source of leverage. As an engine of growth. It is a system of identity and belonging that shapes how people relate to your company and each other.

This book was born from watching dozens of organizations, from early-stage startups to public companies, try to harness that force. Some succeeded. Many didn't. But the ones who did shared something in common: they understood that community isn't a tactic. It's a worldview. It's a decision to invite others into what you're building, and to treat that invitation with seriousness.

If you're picking up this book, chances are you already believe that. You've seen glimpses of what community can do.

Maybe you've built a thriving forum. Perhaps your users have begun to organize themselves. Maybe you've tried to "build community" and found it more complex than expected. Or perhaps you're just curious, because you sense that the next chapter of business will be more human, more participatory, and more networked than the last.

Whatever brought you here, this book is meant to offer you a map, not a blueprint, but a compass. You'll find stories, frameworks, and principles designed to help you build communities that don't just exist, but matter. Communities that don't just support your strategy but become part of it.

You don't need to be a "community manager" to apply what's here. This book is for founders, executives, designers, marketers, product teams, and anyone who believes that people can be more than users. That relationships can be more than transactions. And that trust, when built intentionally, becomes your most defensible advantage.

I hope what you find in these pages is both practical and provocative. I hope it gives you language for what you've felt intuitively. And I hope it helps you build something real.

The future of strategy is not just about data and decisions.

It's people.

Sabir Chatte

Introduction

Chapter 1: Why Community-Led Strategy Matters Now

Business strategy has always been defined by leverage. From the earliest merchant trade routes to the sprawling digital platforms of today, the most successful businesses have found ways to harness existing forces, capital, labor, distribution, data, and technology and multiply their reach. But in the last decade, a new form of leverage has emerged, and it doesn't sit neatly on a balance sheet. It's the leverage of people who care, not just consumers, not just fans, but true believers. It's the collective energy of a community.

You've probably felt this shift yourself, even if you haven't named it. The restaurant that survives not just on great food but on the passionate local following that fills it night after night. The startup whose growth outpaces its ad budget because its users won't stop talking about it. The open-source project evolves faster than most software teams can plan, because its community contributes to both code and culture. These are not just isolated phenomena; they're signals of a broader change in how value is created and how strategy must evolve to capture it.

Community, in this new context, is no longer a nice-to-have. It is not an add-on for marketing, or a social media channel, or a feel-good initiative buried in HR. It is a strategic pillar, a living system that can shape everything from product direction to customer loyalty to brand identity. And when it's nurtured intentionally, when it's aligned with business goals rather than siloed from them, it becomes one of the most potent, defensible assets a company can possess.

Of course, community is not new. Humans have always organized themselves around shared purpose, identity, and need. But what's new, and what demands our attention now, is how digital infrastructure has radically increased our ability to find, nurture, and scale these communities in service of business outcomes. What used to require physical presence, media gatekeepers, or massive capital can now be done by a team of five in a Slack workspace or a Discord server. The barriers are down, the tools are in everyone's hands, and the demand for connection, for contribution, for meaning, is surging.

This is not just about startups or consumer brands. It's happening across industries, across business models, across company stages. Enterprise software companies are building grassroots adoption by empowering user champions. Solopreneurs are turning their audiences into ecosystems. Even traditional organizations, once skeptical of anything that felt "soft," are realizing that community might be their missing moat.

Why now? Because the old playbooks are cracking. Advertising costs are rising. Social algorithms are opaque and fragile. Consumers are savvier, more skeptical, and far less loyal than they were even a decade ago. Trust is no longer distributed from the top down; it's earned sideways, peer to peer, within networks. The brands that win today aren't the ones shouting the loudest, but the ones that become part of the conversation people are already having.

But here's the nuance: building community isn't the same as building an audience. It's not a numbers game. It's not about reach, or followers, or even engagement in the shallow sense. A community is defined not just by its existence, but by the depth of its connections between people, not just to a brand. It's not just how many people show up, but what they do for each other when they get there. And that kind of depth cannot be faked, forced, or bought. It has to be earned.

That's why strategy matters so deeply here. Many businesses have flirted with community, starting groups, hosting events, launching forums, only to watch them sputter out, misunderstood or under-resourced. They thought the community was a marketing channel. They measured it like a funnel. And when it didn't convert the way ads did, they moved on. What they missed is that community isn't a campaign. It's a commitment. And like any strategic asset, it demands clarity, investment, and intention.

This book is about that intention. It's about helping you, whether you're a founder, a strategist, a community lead, or a curious observer, to understand how community can not just support your strategy but *become* it, not as an abstract ideal, but as a practical, repeatable system that integrates with how your business creates, captures, and sustains value.

We'll explore the different types of communities and how they map to other business goals. We'll unpack real case studies, from B2B to creator economy to open-source, that show how community-led strategy works in the wild. We'll walk through frameworks for designing, measuring, and evolving communities in sync with your company's trajectory. And we'll be honest about what it takes, because community, done well, is not free, easy, or quick. But when it works, it's transformative.

If you're reading this, you're likely already convinced that community matters. Maybe you've felt it, or built it, or longed for it. What this book will give you is the strategic language, mental models, and practical tools to make community not just a passion, but a plan.

Because in a world where attention is fragmented, trust is scarce, and change is constant, community isn't just a good idea, it's your most sustainable edge.

The most disruptive businesses today are not those that move the fastest or raise the most money, but those that build the most resilient and loyal ecosystems. You can buy a reach. You can rent attention. But you cannot outsource belonging. And belonging, true, participatory connection, is what communities create. When that belonging is centered within your strategy, it doesn't just support your mission. It becomes the thing that sustains it when everything else gets tested.

This shift has been happening quietly for years. Some of the most influential modern brands, ones that command loyalty far beyond the functional value of their products, have achieved that not through top-down messaging, but through bottom-up energy. Think of Notion, which turned its early users into evangelists by listening obsessively and building in public. Or Duolingo, whose vibrant forum culture and user memes created a sense of shared experience far deeper than most educational apps ever hope to reach. Or Figma, which made design collaboration not just a feature, but a philosophy that turned users into contributors and contributors into a community.

None of these brands started by saying, "Let's build a community." They began by listening and noticing that their users were forming bonds around the product, not just with it. And instead of treating that energy as a side effect, they treated it as the core opportunity. They invested in it, designed it for their needs, and protected it. The result? Growth that was not only faster, but stickier. Cultures that scaled alongside the product, not against it. Moats are built not out of patents, but people.

Of course, community-led strategy isn't just for software. Consider how Patagonia has built a multi-generational coalition of environmentally conscious customers who see the brand not as a retailer, but as a reflection of their values. Or how LEGO re-centered its business around fan builders, adult enthusiasts, and open design competitions, turning consumers into collaborators. Or how CrossFit exploded into a global phenomenon not by perfecting a product, but by empowering an international web of local trainers who carried the culture into their boxes, communities, and cities.

Each of these examples illustrates something profound: that strategy is no longer just about competitive positioning in a market. It's about cultural positioning inside a network. That shift is subtle but seismic. It requires leaders to think not just in terms of supply and demand, or product and market fit, but in terms of meaning, trust, and participation. It means asking: What do our people believe? What do they want to be part of? How can our company give them a role, not just a service?

For many business leaders, these are uncomfortable questions. They sound abstract. Hard to measure. Risky to base decisions on. But the companies that ignore them will be outpaced by the ones that don't. Because today, the fastest-growing organizations aren't just building products, they're building movements. And movements aren't created by algorithms or roadmaps. They're made by people who see themselves in something bigger than themselves.

This is the heart of community-led strategy. It's the recognition that people don't just buy what you make. They join what you're building. And when they feel ownership in that building process, when they see their feedback implemented, their ideas valued, their stories reflected, they stick around. They contribute more. They defend you when things go wrong. They bring others in. They make your brand more than a transaction.

And in doing so, they make your business more than a business.

That might sound idealistic. In some ways, it is. Community, after all, is built on trust, and trust is a fragile, human thing. It can't be forced. It doesn't obey growth targets or quarterly reviews. But that doesn't make it un-strategic. It makes it even more strategic because when you earn trust at scale, when you build something that people want to protect and grow with you, you're no longer just pushing your business forward. You're being pulled forward by the people who care about it.

And in a world where most companies are still fighting for attention, that pull is priceless.

But let's be clear: community is not a shortcut. It's not a magic unlock for hypergrowth. It's not a replacement for a good product, precise positioning, or business fundamentals. What it is, when treated with respect and designed with clarity, is an amplifier. It takes what's already working and deepens it. It takes your story and gives it new voices. It takes your value and distributes it through relationships that no ad campaign could ever buy.

That's why it's so important to approach community-led strategy with rigor, not as a fuzzy set of "vibes," but as a structured discipline. You'll need to think critically about the type of community you're building. About the roles people play. About how contribution happens, how value flows, and how governance evolves, you'll need to define success in ways that go beyond likes and follows, into metrics that reflect absolute trust and real impact.

This book will give you the tools to do that. But first, it will provide you with the mindset. Because strategy isn't just a plan, it's a lens, a way of seeing the world and making choices within it. And the option to center community is not just a tactical one. It's philosophical. It reveals what you believe about business and people. It suggests that people want to be part of something meaningful. That they're not just consumers of value, but producers of it. Your company doesn't just serve a market; it belongs to a community.

When you make that shift, when you truly see your customers, partners, fans, and contributors as a community, not just a collection of users, everything else starts to follow. Your strategy becomes more organic. Your culture becomes more resilient. Your brand becomes more human. And your growth, while it may take longer to build, becomes far harder to break.

That's the promise of community-led strategy. And in the chapters ahead, we'll explore how to realize it, step by step, story by story, strategy by strategy.

But before we go further, we need to clarify something essential: What do we mean by "community"? Because it's one of the most used and most misused words in modern business. And if we don't define it clearly, we risk building everything else on a shaky foundation.

Chapter 2: What We Mean by "Community"

Getting Clear on What We're Building

"Community" is one of the most overused and underdefined words in modern business. It's tossed around in strategy decks, job descriptions, investor calls, and Slack threads with an almost talismanic quality, as if saying it enough times will unlock a sense of connection that magically drives growth. But without clarity, community risks becoming a catch-all term that means everything and, therefore, nothing. If we're going to build a strategy around it, we need to start with precision.

To understand what community means in a strategic sense, we have to draw a line between three related, but distinct, concepts: **audience**, **customer base**, and **community**. Each plays a role in a company's ecosystem, but they operate by different rules. Audiences are people who watch. Customers are people who buy. Communities are people who connect, not just with you.

That last part is crucial. In an audience relationship, the flow is unidirectional: you speak, they listen. You publish; they consume. This can be powerful, especially when your message is strong and your platform is wide. But it is inherently limited. It builds awareness, sometimes even loyalty, but not ownership. There is no sense of participation, no deeper layer of investment beyond passive consumption.

Customers, too, may engage regularly, even enthusiastically. They transact. They review. They return. But that's still not community, not yet. Because the defining trait of a community is not how it connects to *you*, the brand, or the company, it's how it connects *within itself*. A community forms when the people around your product or mission begin to find value in each other. When the connective tissue becomes lateral, not just vertical.

The Network Effect of Belonging

This distinction isn't just semantic, it's structural. In a true community, the relationships between members create value. A customer can stop using your product tomorrow and lose little more than functionality. A community member, on the other hand, has something to lose: connection, identity, and belonging. And because of that, their bond is more resilient. They're not just tied to your product; they're tied to each other.

You can see this clearly in the difference between a social media following and a thriving forum. On Instagram, a brand might have a million followers, each individually connected to the account but isolated from one another. In a forum like Indie Hackers, the members aren't just there to watch; they're there to talk, to ask, to contribute. The value isn't just in what the platform offers them; it's in what they offer each other. The experience improves the more people contribute. That is a network effect. And it's the beating heart of community-led strategy.

What this means in practice is that your job isn't just to broadcast messages or even deliver value. It's to *facilitate* the conditions where members can create value for one another. That might mean designing spaces for interaction, giving them tools to self-organize, or simply getting out of their way at the right moments. The role of a company in a community-led model is less like a broadcaster and more like a host, one who curates the environment, sets the tone, and invites participation, but doesn't dominate the conversation.

Shared Purpose, Not Shared Products

Another key misconception is that communities form simply around usage. The fact that a group of people use the same tool or buy the same product does not necessarily mean they are a community. Sometimes this is true, but not always. True communities aren't built just on shared behavior; they're built on shared purpose. They don't just gather around what they use. They gather around what they *believe*.

Take the example of Harley-Davidson. On the surface, it's a motorcycle company. But its real strength lies in the culture it cultivates, a sense of rebellion, freedom, and Americana. Riders wave to each other on the road not because they bought the same product, but because they believe in the same ethos. It's a social contract, not a product demo. Or look at the early days of Glossier, where the community wasn't just about makeup, it was about a movement toward beauty defined by the user, not by the industry. The product came from the community, not the other way around.

This alignment of purpose creates resilience. Products change. Companies evolve. But when people are bonded by something more profound, such as an identity, a goal, or a value system, they stick together. They defend each other. And they bring others in who resonate with the same signal. That's the foundation of viral growth, not gimmicks or giveaways, but the deep, intuitive pull of shared belonging.

Permission, Participation, and Power

A final point that often gets overlooked is that community is not something a brand can own. You can't control a community in the way you might prevent a brand asset or a marketing channel. You can't dictate its outcomes, script its conversations, or fully predict its evolution. Community is *co-created*. That means participation is voluntary, and power is shared.

This can be uncomfortable for companies used to precision and control. A well-managed sales funnel or ad campaign behaves in predictable ways. Community doesn't. People show up when they care, speak up when they're moved, and drift when they're no longer engaged. You can't force them to stay. But what you *can* do is earn their continued participation by giving them a meaningful role in what you're building.

This is where many community efforts falter. They mistake participation for performance. They build "communities" that are essentially marketing audiences in disguise, where every conversation is directed towards a CTA, every comment is closely monitored for brand alignment, and every interaction is ultimately about extraction, not relationship. That's not community. That's theater.

True community gives people a stake. It trusts them to contribute not just as users, but as co-builders, co-owners, even critics. It gives them room to shape direction, not just respond to it. And while this may feel risky, it is also how the strongest, most enduring forms of loyalty are born. Not from obedience, but from trust. Not from control, but from care.

The Four Archetypes of Strategic Communities

Not all communities are built the same, and not all are suitable for every kind of business. To build with intention, we need to understand the different archetypes of community that exist in the world of strategy. While labels can only go so far, thinking in terms of patterns helps us avoid the mistake of assuming that one type of community will behave like another. It also allows us to be honest about what we're trying to build, and why.

The first archetype is the **community of products**. These are people united by their use of a specific tool, platform, or solution. They are your users, but more than that, they are invested in the tool's evolution. This kind of community often includes power users, early adopters, beta testers, and developers who contribute feedback, feature ideas, or integrations. The strength of this community lies in how closely it connects your product to fundamental human needs. A vibrant product community doesn't just reduce churn; it improves the product itself.

The second is the **community of practice**. This group gathers not around a single product, but around a skill, discipline, or professional identity. Think developers sharing best practices, or content marketers trading insights, or data scientists exploring tools together. Your brand might serve this community, but it doesn't own it, and that's a good thing. If you earn a role here, it means your company is seen not just as a vendor, but as a peer—a contributor to the larger mission of advancing a craft.

Then there's the **community of purpose**. These are people bonded by a mission, a set of values, or a cause bigger than any one company. Patagonia didn't build its community by selling jackets; it did so by standing for environmental responsibility.

Similarly, brands in wellness, education, sustainability, and social impact often find their most profound loyalty not through features or discounts, but by rallying around shared beliefs. In a purpose-driven community, brand loyalty becomes identity alignment. And that's one of the strongest levers of all.

Finally, there's the **community of proximity**. These are local, often geographically bound groups who connect through physical presence or shared space. Think local co-working spaces, meetups, city-based tech ecosystems, or even brand-sponsored pop-up hubs. While digital transformation has enabled scale, the desire for real-world connection has not disappeared. It's resurging. Communities of proximity are often overlooked, but they can create strong, tangible bonds that translate into trust and advocacy far faster than digital-only relationships.

A strong community-led strategy often blends these types. A software company might host a product community online, foster a practice-based Slack for its field, and support in-person meetups in key cities, all while aligning to a broader purpose. The key isn't to choose one as "best," but to understand what kind of relationships you're trying to foster and why. Each type creates value differently, requires different structures, and speaks to a different kind of motivation. The more precise you are about which archetype(s) you're nurturing, the better your chances of building something sustainable.

From Flash Mob to Ecosystem: How Communities Evolve

Many companies misjudge the lifecycle of a community. They treat it like a launch event: something you start with a burst of energy, some branded assets, maybe a landing page or a Discord link, and then wait to see if it "grows." But communities aren't born as communities. They begin as networks, often small, messy, informal, and only over time, through consistent care and interaction, do they cohere into something with identity and memory.

In the early stage, you have a gathering of people around a topic or tool, possibly sharing content or collaborating occasionally. This is fragile. It can disappear quickly if the energy drops or if people don't find reasons to return. Your role in this stage is to facilitate continuity, making it easy to come back, reconnect, and contribute in small but meaningful ways. Too much structure early on can stifle; too little can scatter.

If you succeed in maintaining that gathering, it starts to develop its rituals, norms, and tone. This is the next phase: community as culture. Inside jokes emerge. Language becomes shared. Regulars appear. This is when a group begins to recognize itself as a "we." You'll see members referring to each other by name, calling back to past events, and starting to shape behavior without your prompting. This is a sign that the community has taken root and that your role must begin to shift from host to steward.

Eventually, with enough time and value exchange, a community can evolve into something more robust: a whole ecosystem. This means people are not just participating, they're creating. They're spinning off their projects, hosting their events, and even monetizing their contributions. Your brand becomes one node among many, and the health of the system depends less on your actions and more on the relationships between the other nodes. This is where things can get unpredictable, but also where real strategic upside lives. Because ecosystems can scale in ways that top-down organizations simply can't.

But it's important to recognize that not every group will reach this stage. Nor should they have to. A small, tight-knit user forum can be just as strategically valuable as a massive, decentralized contributor network, if it's aligned to the right goals. The danger is assuming that community success is only measured by size or self-sufficiency. Sometimes, the best communities are the ones that stay small enough to remain human.

Signals of Hype vs Signals of Health

In the rush to "build community," it's easy to chase surface metrics. Member counts, engagement rates, number of posts, or emoji reactions- these can all feel impressive. But metrics do not mean. And hype is not health.

A healthy community isn't just active, it's *cohesive*. Members respond to each other, not just to prompts. Contribution happens voluntarily, not just in response to gamification. Leadership emerges organically. Disagreements happen, but they're handled with mutual respect and shared context. You start to see a kind of immune system forming members who step in to uphold the tone, welcome newcomers, or protect against spam. That's when you know the community has moved beyond you. It is now self-aware. It wants to survive.

On the flip side, unhealthy communities can still be noisy. Sometimes they're even louder than healthy ones. But the energy feels different, more performative, more extractive, more driven by short-term incentives than long-term relationships. You'll notice cliques instead of clusters, complaints instead of contributions, cynicism instead of care. These are signs that something has gone off-track and that strategic intervention is needed, not just a new event or another post, but a return to purpose and trust.

Community as a Living System

To treat community as a strategy, you must treat it as a living system, not a feature to deploy, but an organism to understand. Like any system, a community has flows: of information, attention, value, and trust. These flows must be nurtured, not engineered. You don't force a connection; you make it possible. You don't assign meaning; you make space for it to emerge.

This doesn't mean abandoning structure. But it means choosing structure in the service of life. Too much rigidity and the system suffocates. Too little, and it never coheres. You're aiming for a dynamic structure that provides continuity while being flexible enough to adapt as people change. And people *will* change. Their needs, interests, and availability will shift. What brings them in may not be what keeps them. What keeps them may not be what activates them. Your job is to keep listening.

That's the heartbeat of community-led work: sustained listening. Listening is not just about hearing complaints or collecting testimonials, but about detecting patterns, emotions, and energy. It's one thing to know what your members say. It's another to understand what they *feel* and what they *need*, especially when they haven't said it out loud. Community strategy is pattern recognition in motion.

This is also why community strategy can't be fully outsourced. You can hire great people to facilitate and scale it, but leadership must stay emotionally proximate to it. The further away executives get from the authentic voices of their community, the more likely they are to misunderstand what's happening, and worse, to make decisions that break the very trust they hope to cultivate. If your community becomes something your leadership only hears about in quarterly reports, it will eventually reflect that distance in its energy.

The Question Beneath the Strategy

So, if we strip away the hype, the jargon, the overuse of the word "engagement," what are we talking about when we talk about community?

We're talking about a company's answer to an ancient, very human question: Do I belong here?

That's the question people are always asking, whether silently or explicitly, when they interact with a brand, a product, or a group. It's the question behind their feedback, their participation, their silence. And your community-led strategy is, in many ways, your company's ongoing answer.

When your answer is clear, consistent, and honest, when it says *yes, you belong here, and not just as a buyer, but as a builder*, then the rest begins to follow. People stay. They show up. They take initiative. They give the benefit of the doubt. They forgive mistakes. They invite others in. They invest. Not just their money, but their identity.

That's the real return on community. Not clicks or posts or attendance, but belief. Belief that they matter. Belief that this is worth their time. Belief that what they're part of is, in some small or large way, theirs.

And belief, in the hands of a strategic thinker, is leverage.

In the chapters ahead, we'll build on this understanding. We'll explore how community-led thinking fits into the larger evolution of business strategy, how it compares to product-led and sales-led models, and why it offers something fundamentally different. We'll look at how to structure communities for other strategic goals, how to design for contribution, and how to avoid the traps that make so many community initiatives stall.

But before we build anything, we have to think differently. About people. About value. About the role of business in networks, not just markets.

Because once you start seeing your customers not just as endpoints of a funnel but as nodes in a system, something shifts. The questions get bigger. The upside gets deeper. The responsibility gets heavier.

And the strategy, if you're brave enough to follow it, becomes more human than you ever expected.

Now that we've defined what community means, let's examine how it fits into the broader evolution of business strategy itself.

PART 1: FOUNDATIONS OF COMMUNITY LED THINKING

Reminder: What Makes a Community, Not Just an Audience

Before we go deeper into the strategic mechanics of community-led thinking, let's pause and clarify a key distinction, one that everything else in this section will depend on.

An **audience** is a group of people who pay attention to you. They read your content. They follow your updates. They might even buy what you're selling. But their relationship is mostly one-way. You speak; they listen.

A **community**, by contrast, is a group of people who find value in one another. Their relationship is many-to-many. They don't just show up for you; they show up with and for each other. A community becomes its living system. And that's where the real leverage lies.

Many companies often confuse the two. They measure followers and call it a community. But numbers don't make a network. Connection does.

So as we begin mapping out the structure and strategic value of communities, keep this simple test in mind: **if your people disappeared tomorrow, would they miss you, or would they miss each other?**

If it's the latter, you're building something powerful.

Now let's break down what that power looks like and how to design for it.

Chapter 3: The Evolution of Strategy

Where Business Strategy Comes From

Strategy, at its root, is about where to play and how to win. It's the compass organizations use to focus energy, allocate resources, and make hard choices. For the last fifty years, most business strategies have revolved around two core paradigms: **product-led** and **sales-led** approaches. Each has produced massive success stories. Each made sense in the context of its time. But each is now running into limits.

Sales-led strategy, dominant throughout much of the twentieth century, especially in enterprise and industrial markets, emphasized building strong sales forces, controlling customer relationships, and capturing value through distribution and contracts. The game was often played behind closed doors, through negotiation, exclusivity, and long sales cycles. The company's strategic power came from relationships, reputation, and access.

Then came the internet. Distribution got democratized. Gatekeepers were bypassed. And the product-led era emerged.

In a product-led strategy, the product itself is the growth engine. Design a tool so intuitive and valuable that people can self-serve, adopt quickly, and spread it to others. Think of Dropbox, Slack, Zoom, tools that didn't need a salesperson to explain them. They needed a user to love them. The strategy was rooted in UX, fast iteration, freemium models, and virality through usage.

This shift changed how companies allocated power internally. Product teams became central. Engineers, designers, and growth marketers, often working in lean, cross-functional pods, replaced traditional sales departments as the core engine of scale. The metrics changed, too: CAC and LTV became the gospel; conversion rates were king. Speed and efficiency ruled.

But even this model, agile and effective as it has been, is beginning to show its cracks. The world is noisier now. New tools and products launch every day. Switching costs are low. Differentiation is increasingly difficult. And users, especially younger generations, are less impressed by clever onboarding flows and more motivated by trust, culture, and belonging. It's not enough to be the best-built product anymore. You have to be the product people want to build *with*.

This is where community-led strategy enters. Not as a replacement, but as an evolution. A new dimension of leverage that doesn't negate product or sales but integrates them into a broader human system.

Community-led strategy asks not just: how do we create value and deliver it? But also: who else can co-create this with us? How do we turn users into advocates, customers into contributors, stakeholders into stewards? It flips the question of growth from "how do we scale up our funnel?" to "how do we design for participation?"

This change is subtle at first. A company might launch a forum, a Slack group, or host events. But over time, the shift deepens. Instead of thinking of "target customers," teams start thinking in terms of member journeys. Instead of optimizing for retention through features, they explore how to deepen relationships. Instead of treating support as a cost center, they see it as a stage for reputation, mentorship, and mutual aid.

The fundamental assumption of community-led strategy is that people don't just want solutions; they want to be part of something. And that "something" can become a source of long-term strategic advantage, if it's designed with intention.

When Strategy Becomes Social

The rise of community-led thinking reflects a more profound shift in society: the increasing centrality of social capital. In a time of institutional distrust, algorithmic noise, and constant digital overload, people trust *people*. They listen to peers, not press releases. They follow what their networks love, not what ads tell them to buy. Even the most buttoned-up B2B executive is still a person with an inbox full of LinkedIn messages, a Twitter feed filled with peers, and a subconscious that is tuned to signals from the people they believe in.

Strategy, therefore, must evolve to meet this social reality.

In a traditional model, power is centralized. Value flows outward. Control is top-down. In a community-led model, power is distributed. Value circulates laterally. Leadership is still essential, but it looks more like curation than command.

To operate in this model, companies must learn to work in public. That doesn't just mean tweeting your roadmap or running a community town hall. It means being willing to be seen in the process of becoming, not just showcasing the finished product. It means allowing customers and members to influence outcomes. It means recognizing that control is not the same as strength. Companies that attempt to control their communities often increase their power over them. The strongest communities are those where members feel trusted, empowered, and heard.

This does not mean abdicating responsibility. Community doesn't mean chaos. Strategy is still needed, perhaps more than ever. But it's a different kind of strategy: one that moves at the pace of trust. One that optimizes not just for efficiency or throughput, but for depth of relationship. One that sees every interaction as an opportunity to reinforce identity, not just push toward conversion.

And this is where the most incredible opportunity lies. Because most companies are still operating from the old playbooks, they're optimizing for scale without meaning, reach without resonance. They're throwing money at ads while ignoring the latent power of the people who already care about them.

The community-led strategist sees what others miss: that there is power in participation, and profit in co-creation. That loyalty is no longer just about satisfaction, but about identity. And that in a world of endless options, people don't just want products, they want places to belong.

The Stacking Model of Strategy

Community-led strategy does not erase what came before it. It builds on it. The most successful companies today are not choosing between sales-led, product-led, or community-led; they're stacking these approaches to create layered systems of value and growth. But stacking only works when you understand what each layer is doing and when to activate it.

Sales-led models are particularly effective in high-touch, high-value transactions where human relationships are integral to the deal. Think enterprise software, complex infrastructure, or bespoke consulting services. In these worlds, trust and access are currency. A great salesperson isn't just closing deals; they're educating, de-risking, and personalizing the pitch to navigate an organization's politics and priorities.

That will never go away. But a sales-led strategy alone becomes brittle in the modern era if it's not backed by strong product and strong community signals. Why? Today's buyers do more research on their own, consult more peers, and expect more transparency than ever before. Sales can't carry the load alone.

Then came the product-led era, with its focus on reducing friction and letting the product "sell itself." Here, value is shown, not told. Product-led growth depends on a clean onboarding experience, well-defined usage paths, and metrics-driven iteration. It thrives on speed and clarity. But it, too, has limits. A beautiful product is not always enough to differentiate, especially when competitors can mimic features rapidly. When switching costs are low and attention spans are shorter, what keeps people around is no longer just utility; it's emotional resonance.

Enter the community layer.

Community doesn't replace sales or product. It binds them. It reinforces trust before the sale, accelerates activation after adoption, and deepens loyalty long after purchase. A prospect who hears about you from a friend inside your community comes in warmer. A new user who can ask real humans, not just a chatbot, for help will activate faster. A long-term customer who starts mentoring others in your ecosystem will become far more than a retained account; they will become part of your growth engine.

Think of it like a flywheel. Sales can create initial motion. The product can accelerate it. But the community sustains it, because it introduces energy from sources outside your organization. Your internal teams will always be limited by time and budget. A strong community, however, creates a compounding force, with people creating content, solving problems, telling stories, and building extensions all without you having to ask.

This is why innovative companies don't treat the community as a department. They treat it as a layer of strategic infrastructure. It informs marketing, but it is not *just* marketing. It supports customer success, but it is not *just* support. It drives product development, but it is not *just* feedback. It is the connective tissue that holds all of these functions together, and, at its best, improves how they all operate.

How Companies Shift Into Community-Led Strategy

The transition into a community-led model doesn't happen overnight. It often begins in response to a bottleneck. A company may hit a wall with paid acquisition. Or find that churn is increasing. Or realize that customers are asking for a deeper role in shaping the roadmap. These pain points are often signals that the company has outgrown its old model and needs to make participation a strategic priority.

There are generally three entry points where community-led strategy begins to take root.

The first is in **product feedback**. When early users start sharing detailed suggestions, building workarounds, or creating resources for others, they're expressing something deeper than opinion; they're expressing ownership. If a company listens to and incorporates user feedback and builds mechanisms for users to keep contributing, it plants the seeds of a product community.

If it ignores those signals, or treats them as noise, it misses the chance to build alignment and loyalty.

The second entry point is **peer support**. A growing user base creates surface area for questions, troubleshooting, and education. Many companies begin by answering those questions directly. But over time, as space is created, users start to help each other through forums, Slack channels, and Discord servers. This is the first layer of decentralized value creation. Every time a user answers a question that another might have opened a support ticket for, the company saves money, but more importantly, builds a culture of generosity. Over time, those contributors become unofficial leaders. They need recognition, not just utility.

The third entry point is through **identity and belonging**. Some customers begin to see themselves as more than consumers. They advocate, they teach, they show up again and again. They use your brand as a vehicle for their voice. These are the early signs of a community of purpose. And while not every company will have this kind of relationship with its customers, those who do must be careful with it. Because identity is delicate, if you invite people to see your brand as part of who they are, you must be ready to listen and respond when they tell you how that identity is evolving.

Each of these entry points represents a moment of potential. You can ignore it and remain in a one-directional relationship. Or you can lean in and begin the shift to a community-led mindset. The companies that make this shift successfully often do so quietly at first. They don't launch grand community "initiatives." They show up. They participate. They listen. They empower. Over time, those small actions compound into something larger, an ecosystem with its energy, its norms, its sense of momentum.

Strategic Patience, Long-Term Leverage

The temptation with any new strategy is to measure it by the old standards. Community is no different. Companies often want quick ROI, clear attribution, and linear conversion paths. But community doesn't operate in straight lines. Its value is revealed over time, through reputation, referrals, retention, and resilience. You can't always trace the origin of loyalty, but you feel it in the way people speak about you when you're not in the room.

This doesn't mean community is vague or immeasurable. It simply means you have to measure different things. Instead of clicks, track contributions. Instead of impressions, look at relationships. Instead of one-off sales, look for opportunities to build recurring advocacy. These are the new signals of success. They may be slower to surface, but they're stronger once they appear.

A community-led strategy asks leaders to think beyond the quarter. To plant trees, they should not sit under them. To build infrastructure that compounds, even if it doesn't pay off tomorrow. In a world increasingly obsessed with speed and visibility, this kind of patience is rare. But it's also the kind that builds enduring companies, the kind whose communities don't just use the product, but grow up with it.

From Systems of Control to Systems of Trust

To understand why community-led strategy is gaining momentum, you have to look at what's breaking in traditional models. Most legacy strategies are built on **systems of control**. Control over distribution. Control over brand. Control over messaging. But the digital economy has systematically chipped away at all three. Anyone can distribute. Brand is now co-authored. Messaging spreads through memes and social loops faster than any press release. In this environment, **influence is earned, not owned**.

This makes many executives uneasy. Strategy, as traditionally taught, is about defensible advantage, things others can't copy. Community, by contrast, often feels open, fluid, and messy. But in a trust-based world, **dirty can be more durable than rigid**. Why? Because messy systems bend. They adapt. And when communities are real, when they are rooted in shared values and genuine contribution, they can handle volatility far better than purely transactional customer relationships.

This is why many of the world's most resilient brands today have communities that act as **shock absorbers**. During a PR crisis, it's community members who step in to offer perspective or defend the brand. During product outages or pivots, it's the communities that offer forgiveness when they feel respected. And during moments of cultural tension, it's the community, not comms departments, that often keeps the company grounded in what matters to its people.

Community also becomes the **engine of renewal**. Traditional growth curves often flatten as channels saturate. Paid ads get more expensive. SEO gets more competitive. Outreach becomes white noise. But in a community-led model, growth becomes **organic**, driven by relationships, not just tactics. Every new contributor brings not just value, but more surface area for discovery. Every shared story becomes a node of distribution. And every small gathering becomes a seedbed for more.

That's why community-led strategy isn't a phase. It's not a trend to ride. It's a new lens, one that reveals different kinds of leverage and invites a different type of leadership.

Leadership in the Age of Participation

The leadership required for community-led strategy is different from that required in previous eras. It's less about control and more about **curation**. Less about command and more about **consistency**. The best community-led leaders are not always the loudest. They are often the most generous with credit, the most skilled at listening, and the most comfortable with ambiguity.

This doesn't mean leadership disappears. Communities without leadership often drift, fragment, or become dominated by the loudest voices. But the leadership that works in this context is rarely top-down. It's **network-aware**, capable of recognizing influence wherever it lives, and lifting those who make the community better, not just bigger.

For many companies, this requires a mindset shift. Leaders must be willing to **give up control in exchange for trust**, to listen more than they speak, and to build teams not just of executors, but of facilitators. This is hard work. But the reward is immense: a community that scales your impact, expands your reach, and evolves with your customers, not just for them.

A New Strategic Frontier

As we close this chapter, it's worth emphasizing that community-led strategy is not just a tactical decision. It's a philosophical one. It requires seeing your company not just as a service provider, but as a **platform for belonging**. It requires trusting that value can emerge from co-creation, not just consumption. And it demands patience, a willingness to invest in relationships that may take time to reveal their full return.

But make no mistake: this is a strategy. It is as deliberate, structured, and impactful as any market analysis or sales model. And for those who take it seriously, it can become a durable source of advantage. Not because it's fast. But because it's real.

In the chapters ahead, we'll begin building out the components of this strategy, starting with the anatomy of a strategic community. We'll examine the roles people play, the structures that support participation, and the metrics that help you determine whether your project is thriving.

Because while community may start with connection, strategy begins with design.

And now, it's time to design something built to last.

Chapter 4: The Anatomy of a Strategic Community

I've worked with companies that thought they had a community because they had thousands of email subscribers. Others had built Discord servers, set up badges, even hired community managers, but still couldn't explain what their community was *for*. The surface activity was there. The underlying structure wasn't.

After watching dozens of organizations wrestle with this, it became clear: most teams don't fail at community because of a lack of intent. They fail because they skip the anatomy.

Community is not a vibe. It's not a place. It's a system. And like any system, it has parts, roles, relationships, and flows of value. The companies that build strong communities know how to name these parts, design for them, and evolve them over time. That's what we're going to do in this chapter.

But before we break it down, let's reconnect to what brought us here.

In Chapter 3, we talked about the evolution of business strategy, from sales-led to product-led to community-led. We framed community as the connective tissue, the layer that adds resilience and depth. Now, we'll zoom in and ask: what is that tissue made of? How do you know if you're building something that can live and grow, not just attract people, but hold them?

To answer that, let's start with a metaphor I often use when advising teams.

The Core Elements of Strategic Community Design

With that image in mind, let's define the major structural elements you'll need to design for.

First: **member roles**. Not everyone plays the same part in a community. Some are listeners. Some are contributors. A few become leaders, stewards, or creators. A good community strategy doesn't try to force everyone into contribution; it simply makes it *possible*. Contribution must be optional, not obligatory, or it burns people out. But when someone *chooses* to engage more deeply, the infrastructure should be there to support them.

I once helped a startup where a user kept answering questions faster than the support team. He wasn't on payroll. He wasn't asked to do it. But he had a sense of ownership, and that ownership was met with recognition. They eventually gave him a community title, early product access, and, crucially, *trust*. That person went on to help onboard hundreds of new users. All because there was room for him to lead.

Next: **rituals and rhythms**. Communities need more than a place; they need *time*. Regular events, discussions, check-ins. These don't have to be synchronous. A monthly AMA, a weekly prompt, a quarterly summit, what matters is consistency. Rituals give people a reason to return and a sense of progress over time.

Third: **identity signals**. These can be subtle, such as a naming convention, a shared phrase, a member badge, or even an inside joke. Anything that helps someone say, "I am part of this." These signals don't just bond people; they shape behavior. When people identify with a group, they often show up as their best selves *on behalf of it*.

And finally: **value loops**. This is the most essential element of all. A community must create value not just from you to them, but from **them to each other**. And it must give back in return. Contribution must feel rewarded, even if not financially. Attention, reputation, and access are currencies. If someone's effort disappears into a void, they'll stop giving it. If they feel seen, they'll give more.

The mistake many companies make is assuming they need to do more. Often, it's about doing **less, but with better feedback loops**. Listen louder. Respond faster. Celebrate more publicly. Make it easy for value to circulate, not just accumulate in a brand-owned vault.

Communities Aren't Born Strategic; They Become It

Early-stage communities are messy. They don't follow best practices. They grow in fits and starts. That's okay. What matters in those moments isn't perfection, it's **attunement**. Are you noticing what people are already doing? Are you building scaffolding around behavior that you want to happen?

I've seen companies waste six months building community platforms from scratch when all their members wanted was a group chat and a shared folder of resources. Strategy isn't about complexity. It's about making intentional choices that align your structure with your purpose.

In the chapters ahead, we'll explore how to do just that: how to map your community to specific business goals, how to measure what matters, and how to scale without losing soul.

But before we optimize or measure, we need to build with care. And care starts with clarity. Clarity about what you're building, why people would stay, and what makes this more than just another Slack group.

Because when you get the anatomy right, everything else — growth, culture, and impact —becomes easier to evolve.

Different Community Types, Different Designs

It's tempting to believe there's a universal blueprint for community design, one golden playbook that works across every industry, every audience, every platform. There isn't.

What works beautifully for a developer network may fall flat for a fitness coaching tribe. A consumer product community thrives on emotional identity and shared culture, while a B2B SaaS practice group might rely entirely on peer support and recurring learning.

This is why your community's **anatomy must match its purpose**. It's not just about what tools you use or what content you share; it's about **how people experience connection and value**, and what kinds of behaviors your structure makes possible.

Let's walk through each of the four strategic community archetypes introduced earlier, **product**, **practice**, **purpose**, and **proximity**, and look at what each one requires from a design and participation standpoint.

1. Communities of Product: Built Around Use

These are communities centered around a tool, platform, or product. Consider tools like Notion, Airtable, Figma, or Webflow. The people who join these communities are here for support, innovation, and shared mastery.

Structure here is about surfacing knowledge and rewarding contributions. Your architecture should highlight expert users, create searchable archives of answers, and foster channels for feedback to flow from user to product team. This type of community thrives on clarity, clear roles, clear guidelines, and clear ways to rise through contribution.

I once worked with a design tool that struggled to activate its early user base. The team was frustrated that engagement was flat, despite thousands of signups. But when we asked users directly, they told us: "I don't know where to start." We didn't need a new campaign. We required an orientation ritual. Within a month, we launched a "First 10 Days" experience: one welcome email, one tip, one task per day. Engagement jumped. Contribution followed. Sometimes, structure is just scaffolding for confidence.

2. Communities of Practice: Built Around a Craft

Here, members aren't tied together by one product; a shared discipline unites them. Developers. Content marketers. Data scientists. Designers. These people come together to improve their craft, stay sharp, and connect with others who speak their professional language.

The anatomy of a practice community is about dialogue and peer elevation. What you design must enable shared insight, not just Q&A, but deep, additive discussion. People come for value, but they stay for respect.

In practice communities, hierarchy must be subtle. Expertise matters, but overt gamification often backfires. Instead of points or badges, try thoughtful curation. Elevate thoughtful threads by spotlighting member posts in your newsletter. Make contribution visible but not performative.

One thing to watch: practice communities tend to resist brand intrusion. If you're a company building one, **your role is to host, not dominate**. When done well, your brand becomes a generous facilitator, not a vendor pushing its agenda.

3. Communities of Purpose: Built Around a Belief

These are communities driven by mission. They exist not just to support a product or share knowledge, but to pursue a deeper goal. Climate action. Financial independence. Women in tech. Open education. Purpose communities can be the most emotionally resonant, and the most fragile.

The anatomy here is different. **Belonging becomes the central structure.** The spaces you design should invite identity, storytelling, and reflection. Think rituals, shared language, and member spotlights. People need to feel *seen*.

But purpose without structure can drift into chaos, or worse, burnout. People often give more in mission-driven communities, and if they don't see that energy going anywhere, they leave discouraged. Design clear ways for members to engage meaningfully, set boundaries to protect emotional labor, and **close the loop** between intention and impact.

The best purpose-driven communities I've seen didn't have the most features. They had the strongest **trust loops**. Leaders listened. Members shaped direction. And every contribution, no matter how small, was made to feel like it mattered.

4. Communities of Proximity: Built Around Place

Despite everything we've said about digital scale, **geography still matters**. Communities rooted in location, whether neighborhood co-ops, city-based meetups, or brand-specific chapters, require structures that reflect physical presence, spontaneity, and localized trust.

In these cases, anatomy means logistics: **calendars, venues, safety guidelines, and organizer roles.** You're not just managing content; you're managing *human choreography.* The rituals you create must account for real time, real movement, and real energy levels.

Proximity communities thrive on empowerment. You can't centrally manage every local chapter. So instead, build toolkits. Train facilitators. Trust your people with frameworks, not scripts. Let them remix the brand to fit their context, as long as the values stay consistent.

One of the most vibrant examples I've seen was a fitness brand that not only allowed its members to host workouts but also encouraged them to do so. They gave starter kits, Spotify playlists, and shared sign-up templates. Suddenly, what had been a top-down brand turned into a global patchwork of shared culture. Community became motion. Strategy followed energy.

Design by Type, but Lead by Listening

Understanding your archetype helps you design smarter. But no archetype is static. Many communities blend types over time. A product community begins to develop a purpose, or a practice network evolves into a proximity chapter system.

What matters most is that you're **paying attention to how people are behaving**, not just how you intended them to act.

If your members are starting to help each other without prompting, consider building support tools. If they're talking about their values, elevate that purpose. If they want to meet in person, don't dismiss it; facilitate it.

This is where anatomy becomes strategy: when you let the structure adapt not just to what you offer, but to what your members *need next.*

Seeing Your Community as a System

If you want your community to be more than a crowd, you have to start treating it like a system. And systems can be mapped, not with spreadsheets or dashboards, but through thoughtful observation. What most teams lack isn't data; it's perspective. They describe their communities in vague, reactive terms. They say things like, "It feels quiet," or "It's active lately," or "Engagement's down," without knowing what any of that means.

I've seen companies stay stuck for months simply because they never stopped to ask, "How does this work?" Not metaphorically. Functionally. Who shows up? What do they do when they get here? Who do they talk to? What keeps them coming back? What causes them to leave?

That's where the work of community design begins, when you start to see not just a group of people, but the **relationships, roles, rhythms, and frictions** that make the whole thing move, or stall.

Start by looking for the spark. Every community has one. It's that first moment when someone feels like they belong. Sometimes it's a warm welcome from a real person. Sometimes it's discovering a thread that speaks directly to their situation. Sometimes it's the quiet comfort of seeing others like them, navigating the same road. That first moment of recognition matters more than most teams realize. If people join and see nothing but silence, they quietly disappear. If they get dropped into a space with no context, no warmth, no cues, they don't say anything. They leave. And they don't come back.

The spark doesn't have to be flashy. It just has to feel intentional. A simple note from another member. A pinned post that orients newcomers. A moment of validation, however small. The earlier that moment arrives, the more likely someone is to stay.

Once you know where the spark is, shift your attention to the energy. Every community has certain people who show up even when no one asks them to. They start conversations, answer questions, organize meetups, or respond thoughtfully when others don't. These people are your informal leaders, not by title, but by presence. They carry the energy of the community, often without being asked.

But energy has a cost. If you rely on these people without supporting them, they'll burn out. I've seen it happen too many times. One or two members become the heart of the space, and when they quietly disappear, the pulse flatlines. You have to make sure the people driving energy are also receiving it. That can be as simple as recognizing their effort, asking for their input, or creating roles that give them more ownership without burying them in responsibility. The structure should lift them, not lean too hard on them.

Next, look at how value moves. In a healthy community, value doesn't just flow from the brand to the members; it circulates among the members themselves. People share advice, tell stories, post resources, and celebrate each other's wins. The community becomes not just a place to receive, but a place to contribute. And that contribution becomes part of the reward.

The circulation of value is one of the most evident signs that you've built something real. If every meaningful interaction still depends on your team initiating it, the system hasn't taken root. But if people are helping each other, building things together, referring friends, or riffing off each other's ideas, that's a system in motion. You're no longer the sole source of momentum. You've created something that sustains itself, at least in part, through its internal gravity.

Still, even vibrant systems can struggle with friction. Often, when communities slow down or stagnate, it's not because people don't care. It's because they're quietly bumping into obstacles. Maybe the onboarding is confusing. Perhaps no one responds to posts. Maybe the space feels dominated by a few loud voices, or the culture is unclear, or the tooling doesn't match the energy.

These frictions don't always announce themselves. They creep in quietly. A new member joins, can't figure out what to do, and fades away. A core contributor gets tired of posting into silence and pulls back. Over time, those little moments add up, not with drama, but with erosion.

So, look for the places where effort goes unrewarded. Look for moments of hesitation. Pay attention to what's being tolerated but not talked about. Some friction is useful; it creates norms, sets expectations, and keeps standards high. But there's a difference between friction that shapes behavior and friction that drains it.

And finally, notice how people evolve. In the best communities, members don't stay stuck in one role forever. They grow. A quiet observer becomes a participant. A regular contributor becomes a leader. A leader mentors someone new. These transitions don't always happen on a schedule, but they should be possible. If everyone remains a passive consumer, the structure might be too closed or too opaque. People need to see not only what they can do today, but what they might grow into tomorrow.

Communities, like organizations, thrive on clear paths to contribution. But those paths must feel earned, not assigned. People want to feel they've stepped into something because they chose it. After all, it felt like the right moment, the right fit. If you push too hard, they resist. If you don't make the invitation clear, they never move.

Once you begin to understand all of this — where the spark lives, where the energy comes from, how value circulates, where the friction hides, and how roles evolve — you can start designing from truth, not theory. You can stop guessing at what might work and start reinforcing what already wants to happen.

In the next chapter, we'll take this one step further. We'll explore how communities generate business outcomes, not just through warm vibes or good intentions, but through real strategic loops. We'll look at how participation compounds, how momentum becomes growth, and how contribution drives insight, loyalty, and scale.

Because when you design a community that works, you haven't just built a nice brand asset. You've built a growth engine.

Chapter 5: The Community Flywheel

In the earliest days of a community, the energy required to sustain it often feels disproportionate to the outcome. You find yourself starting every thread, responding to every comment, and sending each follow-up email by hand. You're not managing momentum, you're manufacturing it. Nothing moves unless you do.

This isn't failure. It's how living systems begin, small, deliberate, and intimate. But over time, if the design is right, something starts to shift—a regular member posts without prompting. A familiar voice greets someone new before you get the chance. Questions begin to generate answers from places you didn't expect. What once required constant ignition now begins to rotate under its own force.

That shift, subtle at first and then unmistakable, is the beginning of what I've come to call the community flywheel. It's the moment when the community transitions from effort to rhythm. The turning doesn't stop, but it starts to **carry itself**. And with every new rotation, the weight of trust, connection, and value builds a kind of strategic gravity that becomes harder to replicate with any other method.

The flywheel isn't a trend or a tactic. It's a structural pattern, one that reveals how communities evolve from fragile beginnings into durable, compounding systems. It begins with something small: an act of participation. Someone decides to show up, not as a customer following instructions, but as a person choosing to contribute. Maybe they post a question, share an experience, or thank someone publicly. That action, however small, becomes the wheel's first turn.

From there, value emerges. Not always immediately, and not always evenly, but participation, when held well, tends to generate something in return. It might be a helpful answer. It might be a conversation that wasn't expected. It might simply be the feeling of being acknowledged. Over time, as those exchanges multiply, something else begins to build: trust. Not just in the brand or platform, but in the people. In the space itself. In the culture that's taking shape.

And it's that trust that lies at the foundation of commitment. Once people feel both welcome and respected, believing their voice belongs and their time matters, they start to return with intent and begin sharing more openly. They invite others. They step forward, sometimes quietly, into deeper forms of contribution.

The wheel, now in motion, doesn't just repeat; it strengthens. Each new act of participation reinforces the ones before it. Each moment of value deepens the experience. Each signal of trust makes the next one easier to offer. And slowly, sometimes imperceptibly, the community shifts from a thing you support to a thing that supports itself.

But this momentum doesn't happen by accident. It occurs because the system has been shaped to allow it.

When I first noticed this pattern, it wasn't in a chart or a theory; it was in a product community struggling to scale. Their Slack workspace was chaotic. The forums were half-active, mostly reactive. The support team was exhausted. Yet beneath the surface, a handful of users kept showing up, offering help, sharing templates, answering the same questions again and again without ever being asked.

At first, the company saw these moments as a pleasant surprise. But eventually, someone asked the right question: what if *this* is the engine? What if these behaviors aren't just community side-effects, but the core of our growth?

So, they stopped focusing on surface metrics and started reinforcing those behaviors. They responded to top contributors faster. They elevated thoughtful posts. They invited a few members into roadmap conversations. They didn't bribe them or script them; they **trusted them with the process**.

And the result wasn't a spike in engagement. It was something better: the slow, steady hum of participation becoming culture.

This is the flywheel in practice. Not a diagram. A rhythm.

It's easy to mistake community momentum for marketing success. A well-timed launch, a viral campaign, a surge in traffic. But those are sparks, not systems. The flywheel isn't about bursts; it's about rotation. It doesn't rely on loudness. It depends on repetition. Each member who shows up and is met with care adds a little more force to the wheel. Each act of generosity, when mirrored by recognition, adds another turn.

The question is not whether you can push the wheel. The question is: **have you removed enough friction for it to turn on its own?**

In the next section, we'll explore how to design for each phase of the flywheel, not as a funnel, not as a growth hack, but as a human system. We'll look closely at participation, value, trust, and commitment, not as buzzwords, but as design challenges. Because when the loop works, growth doesn't just happen faster. It happens with more meaning, more retention, and more soul.

And it's that kind of growth, the kind powered by people, not tactics, that scales not just businesses, but belief.

Designing the Loop That Turns Itself

If the community flywheel begins with participation, then your role as a builder is not to manufacture energy, but to lower the cost of showing up. Participation is fragile at first. People hover before they speak. They read before they write. They hesitate before they engage. In many cases, the difference between a thriving community and a stalled one lies in how those first moments are handled.

I've watched spaces stall not because they lacked value, but because they failed to respond. Someone takes the risk of posting a question or sharing an insight. And nothing comes back. No comment. No reply. Not even a like. And so that moment, the potential start of a loop, evaporates.

Incentives don't drive participation. It's driven by response. When people feel acknowledged, they return. And if they return often enough, their contributions begin to form the texture of the community itself.

But participation alone isn't enough. It must generate **value**, and not just in the form of correct answers or clever replies. Value in a community context is emotional as well as informational. It's the experience of feeling useful, of being seen, of receiving something you didn't expect but immediately recognize as meaningful.

Some communities surface value by creating high-quality content. Others do it through dialogue. Still others, through atmosphere alone, have a sense that being here sharpens you, grounds you, or reminds you who you are. There is no one right way. But value, whatever form it takes, must be visible. It must be felt. If it's not, the loop loses tension. People return less often. The cadence softens. The hum dies out.

In one network I worked with, a community for design leaders, we noticed a curious pattern. Members were attending events, but engagement between them was low. Conversations felt flat. Threads stalled early. At first, we assumed people were just busy. But the more profound truth was more straightforward: value was being experienced individually, not collectively. People were attending and learning, but they weren't learning from each other.

The shift occurred when we shifted our focus from guest speakers to designing for reflection. After each event, we prompted members to share a takeaway, not to perform, but to process. We asked questions like, "What will you try differently next week?" or "What surprised you about what was said?" Over time, these small acts of shared meaning created a current. The value became shared. And the loop began to turn.

That shared value becomes the raw material for the next phase: **trust**.

Trust is the most invisible and most powerful layer of the flywheel. It's also the least quantifiable. You can't A/B test your way into trust. It accumulates slowly, and it can be lost in a single moment. But when it's present, it multiplies the impact of everything else.

A trusted community doesn't just attract members, it holds them. It becomes a space where people let down their guard, offer help without needing to posture, admit what they don't know, or share things they haven't voiced elsewhere. Trust is what turns audiences into collaborators. It's what allows feedback to be generous rather than performative. And it's what transforms a transactional space into a relational one.

But trust isn't built solely by tone or kindness. It's built by consistency. People trust what feels stable. They trust what reflects their values. They trust what protects its boundaries, honors its members, and handles tension with care. That means setting expectations, responding when norms are challenged, and modeling the behavior you want to see. Not once, but every time.

In one instance, I observed a fledgling entrepreneurial community struggling after a few aggressive members took over every thread. The team hesitated to intervene. They were afraid of appearing controlling or losing momentum. But silence, in that moment, wasn't neutral; it was a signal. It told quieter members that this was the tone of the space, and if it didn't work for them, they could leave. Many did.

Eventually, the team course-corrected. They clarified expectations. They elevated different kinds of voices. They didn't ban the loud contributors, but they reshaped the space so that others could re-enter. Trust returned, slowly. But the delay had cost them. Culture, once ceded, is hard to reclaim.

And yet, when trust is present, it leads naturally to the final phase of the flywheel: **commitment**.

Commitment isn't just attendance. It's an emotional investment. It's the shift from "this is useful to me" to "this is part of who I am." People begin to identify not just with the value, but with the space itself. They recommend it. They shape it. They bring others in. And, crucially, they stay, even when it's not immediately rewarding, even when the thread doesn't get a reply, even when life gets busy.

That kind of staying power is rare. It's what most brands spend millions trying to simulate with loyalty programs and marketing automation. But in a true community, it happens organically, because the investment is real. It's not gamified. It's earned.

And once commitment shows up, the loop starts to feel inevitable. Members become stewards. Stewards become catalysts. New members feel the energy, reflect it, and join the current. The flywheel no longer needs to be pushed. It turns because people believe in where it's going.

This is not a moment to take lightly. When a community starts turning on its force, your job changes. You move from initiator to amplifier. From builder to curator. From center to supporter.

But first, you have to build the conditions for it to turn.

What Disrupts the Flywheel, and How to Restart It

For all its elegance, the community flywheel is not self-perpetuating forever. It has torque, but it also has drag. And like any living system, it can stall, quietly, suddenly, or gradually over time.

Sometimes it slows because one phase weakens. Participation dries up. Fewer people post, energy dips. You check in and find the same three members carrying the weight they've held for too long. Without new voices, the room echoes. And even the loyal ones begin to drift.

Other times, the value disappears. Conversations get repetitive. Content gets stale. Feedback stops flowing. What once felt generative now feels predictable. The network still exists, but the current is gone. People aren't angry, they're bored.

Most dangerously, the trust erodes. A conflict goes unaddressed. A contributor leaves without explanation. Someone speaks up and hears nothing back. These moments accumulate in silence. They are rarely explosive. But over time, they hollow out the sense of belonging. Members begin to question whether this is a place they can still show up honestly, or at all.

When the flywheel stalls, most teams react tactically. They launch a campaign. Host an event. Offer an incentive. And sometimes, those things help. But more often, they act like sugar, spikes of activity that don't restore the core metabolism.

The better approach is diagnostic. You return to the loop. You ask, softly but clearly: where has participation become harder? Where is the value no longer being surfaced? Where has trust been strained? What was once happening easily that now requires effort?

In one organization I supported, the community had thrived for nearly two years, with high engagement, active members, and natural growth. Then, almost imperceptibly, it began to cool. Fewer posts. More passivity. The core contributors were still there, but the spark was missing.

Rather than chase new signups or layer in gamification, we paused. We spoke directly with long-term members. We asked not what was wrong, but what had changed. And the answer surprised us: it wasn't that anything was broken. The **meaning had drifted**.

The purpose that once animated the group had evolved, but the structure hadn't. The conversations hadn't kept up with the community's maturity. People were solving more complex problems, but the prompts were still at a beginner level. The design no longer matched the depth of the members.

So, we adjusted. We re-framed the conversations. Invited more advanced peer-led sessions. Refreshed the story the community told about itself. And slowly, the hum returned, not with a splash, but with a re-tuning of rhythm. The loop began to turn again, not faster, but more truthfully.

What this revealed, and what I've seen elsewhere, is that the flywheel is never static. It doesn't just spin or stop. It **breathes**. It stretches. It contracts. And when it falters, the work is not to force it forward, but to realign the elements that made it turn in the first place.

This is the subtle but critical truth: momentum is not the goal. Integrity is. A flywheel that turns because people genuinely care, because their contributions are meaningful, because their trust is earned, that loop will outlast any campaign. And when it slows, it can be restarted because its foundation is still intact.

As a builder, your role isn't to optimize every moment. It's to stay close enough to the system to feel its temperature. To sense when participation is hesitant. To notice when the value needs to be redefined. To hold trust as a renewable resource, and treat commitment not as a metric, but as a gift.

And when you do that, when the wheel turns not through force, but through alignment, you're no longer running a program. You're tending to a living structure.

In the next chapter, we'll move inward. We'll explore what makes people **choose to give**, not just attend. We'll look at the architecture of contribution, why it happens, how to support it, and how ownership reshapes the very idea of community.

While the flywheel creates the motion, it is its contribution that shapes the future.

Chapter 6: Community as Moat

Why Moats Matter More Than Ever

Every business eventually reaches the same question: *What protects us?*

Not what grows us. Not what launches us. Not what markets or sells or even delights. But what keeps someone from copying us, outpacing us, or pricing us into irrelevance?

In a crowded market, growth gets you attention. But **defensibility** keeps you alive.

Historically, defensibility came from access. If you had the factory, the patent, the data set, and the distribution, you had the moat. In the digital era, the terrain changed. Moats became more complicated to see and easier to cross. A better UI, a cheaper price, and a clever onboarding loop were all designed to last, but none of these lasted long. Features are copied. Funnels converge, differentiation decays.

Which is why today, the most powerful moats are not technical. They are relational.

And among relational moats, none are deeper, more durable, or harder to replicate than **community**.

A product can be cloned. A price can be undercut. But **trust takes time**, and trust that lives between people, not just between customer and company, is almost impossible to replicate at speed.

That's the crux of community-as-moat. It's not about volume. It's about **density**. The strength of ties. The frequency of interaction. The emotional weight of being seen, responded to, and remembered. It's about how many reasons a person has to stay, not just because the product is good, but because *they feel part of something that would be hard to re-create elsewhere.* We don't often use the word loyalty anymore in business strategy. It sounds outdated, sentimental. But loyalty, in this context, is not just about repeat usage. It's about **identity lock-in**, the subtle, powerful effect of feeling like a user is not just using your tool, but shaping your future. And that their future is entangled with yours.

That entanglement is a strategic asset. It reduces churn. It reduces CAC. It increases time-to-trust with new customers, because the early signals, the reviews, the stories, the mentions, are all human, not scripted. The company doesn't have to tell its own story. The community does it for them.

But more than anything, a strong community makes the company more challenging to compete with, not because of scale, but because of **network effects grounded in shared identity.**

Imagine two companies with similar products. One has thousands of users. The other has a few hundred members. But the first group is silent. Transactional. Anonymous. The second is vibrant. Members engage in discussions, create content, reference each other, and collaborate. They've built artifacts, language, and rituals. When someone leaves, others notice. When someone joins, others welcome.

Which company is harder to disrupt?

Most investors would say the second. Not because it's bigger, but because it's **stickier**. Stickier emotionally, culturally, and strategically. And that stickiness is what gives the company room to breathe. Room to grow without panicking. Room to charge more, take risks, be different, because they're not just selling a product. They're holding a **networked identity**.

In that sense, community isn't just defensibility. It's *permission*. It buys you time. It gives you grace. It earns you the benefit of the doubt in a market that otherwise rewards sameness.

But this kind of community doesn't emerge by accident. It has to be designed, not just for engagement, but for **interdependence**. It has to reward not just participation, but memory. It has to favor **connection over consumption** and build the kind of culture where value is not just distributed, but **co-owned**.

In the next section, we'll explore the mechanics behind that kind of defensibility, how trust builds density. How shared language becomes resistance to churn. And how, over time, **community identity becomes strategic insulation**, not because it keeps others out, but because it makes it harder for your members to want to leave. Because the most powerful moat isn't a wall. It's a *web*.

Trust, Identity, and the Density That Defends

Trust is not a feature. It doesn't show up in onboarding flows or product dashboards. You can't toggle it on. You can't A/B test your way to it. But over time, it becomes the most valuable and least portable asset a company can build.

Unlike speed, cost, or even satisfaction, **trust compounds**. It gets stronger the longer it holds. The more interactions that go well. The more stories that get told. The more members who don't just show up once but stay, the better. Not out of obligation. But out of **alignment**.

And that's what makes trust a moat. It's slow to earn. Deep to embed. And nearly impossible to fast-follow. Even if your competitor copies your UX pixel-for-pixel, they can't import your community's trust because trust lives in the *spaces between people*, not in the features they use.

I once advised a platform team that had been obsessing over retention metrics for months. Their churn looked fine, but they knew something was off. People signed up, used the product, and then… drifted. Quietly. Politely. No complaints. Just departure.

But buried in their support logs and forum archives was the real story: people weren't leaving because the product was broken. They were leaving because **they didn't feel seen**. Their feedback disappeared into a void. Their suggestions got canned replies. No one remembered their names. There were no "insiders," no rituals, no reasons to return beyond utility. And when a cheaper tool launched, they left.

Contrast that with another product in the same category: similar features, slower development, arguably worse UI. But the team knew their users. They used their names. They referenced old threads. They let users vote on roadmap features and followed up. Members of the community got early access. Got thanked publicly. Got remembered.

That company had a worse product, but a more substantial moat. Not because their tech was better, but because their **relationships were genuine**.

Trust creates insulation. But it doesn't stand alone. It works hand-in-hand with something more complex: **identity**.

When someone begins to identify with a community, their sense of self becomes entangled with their presence in a shared space, making leaving emotionally expensive. They don't just lose access. They lose a part of their narrative. A routine. A recognition loop. And identity is far more enduring than incentive.

Incentives can be matched. Badges copied. Points cloned. But **belonging**, the felt sense that "this is where I grow, where I'm seen, where I contribute", that's the stickiest value of all.

This is why community-led companies tend to survive pricing wars and feature parity. They're not just selling functionality. They're anchoring identity. And when a member's story becomes interwoven with your brand, they don't churn when a new tool emerges. They stay. Or even if they leave, they stay loyal to the story. They keep talking about you and recommending you. Returning.

This is the *moat within the moat*. Not just trust in service. But **identity in a relationship**.

So how does that identity take shape?

Often, through **ritual**, the shared rhythms make a space feel lived-in. A weekly roundup. A naming convention. An emoji shorthand that only insiders get. These are not superficial flourishes. They are **cultural signals**. They say, "We know each other here." They allow the community to be not just helpful, but *self-aware*.

And once that happens, defensibility is no longer about what the company does for the customer.

It's about what the community *does for each other*.

In the next section, we'll explore how this peer-to-peer dynamic becomes the real shield: the moment when value stops flowing *from* the center and begins to emerge *between* the members, creating a mesh that no competitor can easily displace, because it wasn't centralized to begin with.

That's the moment the community stops being a moat around the company. And starts becoming the *terrain it's built on.*

Peer-to-Peer Networks as Strategic Terrain

There's a quiet moment in every mature community when something shifts. It's subtle at first, a question answered not by staff, but by another member. A new person was welcomed before the moderators arrived. A resource built not by the core team, but by someone with no formal role. You notice it when you look closely, but more often you feel it, like a current in the room has changed direction.

That shift is the moment a community begins to generate **peer-to-peer value**, when the connections between members become more valuable than the connection to the brand.

And this is where the deepest moat begins to form.

When members rely on each other, when they show up not just to consume value but to **create and exchange it**, the community moves from a channel to an ecosystem. From a space to a system. From something hosted to something *inhabited.*

This kind of interdependence is rare and incredibly difficult to replicate. Because it doesn't depend on perks, promotions, or automation, it depends on **relational gravity**. People stay not because the product keeps them, but because *other people keep them.*

And no competitor can offer that.

Even if they replicate your features, undercut your price, or launch a more polished platform, they can't replicate the feeling of shared history. They can't manufacture mutual trust. They can't port over inside jokes, recurring rituals, or the lived texture of collective presence.

That's the difference between brand community and **community-as-terrain**. In the former, the company is still the center of gravity. In the latter, the community is *the geography itself*. Members navigate, build, and make meaning on their terms. And when that happens, defensibility is no longer maintained by what you own. It's maintained by what they *hold together*.

I've watched this happen in niche developer communities, design forums, and even highly technical SaaS ecosystems. At first, the value comes from the company, tutorials, updates, and product leadership. But over time, that value begins to decentralize. Community-built templates outperform official docs. Member-hosted events pull higher attendance than company webinars. Experts emerge, not because they were appointed, but because they earned attention by showing up, again and again, with clarity and care.

The company, wisely, steps back, not out of disengagement, but out of trust. They become stewards instead of orchestrators, curators instead of controllers. And the system doesn't collapse, it expands.

Because at the heart of all defensible communities is this principle: **value moves from the edges in**.

A healthy community doesn't just rely on the company for value. It reflects it, refracts it, redistributes it. Members become nodes. And as those nodes connect, the entire system becomes more resilient. More generative. More resistant to disruption.

That's network effect, not as a buzzword, but as **behavior**.

And here's the most strategic part: as peer-to-peer ties strengthen, switching costs increase, but *not artificially*. There's no lock-in, no manipulation. There's a growing sense that leaving this place would mean losing something more than just functionality. You'd lose relationships. Rhythm. Recognition. A set of practices, memories, and ongoing conversations that can't be exported.

That's a moat no spreadsheet can quantify, but every operator, founder, or investor can feel.

And that feeling is powerful enough to change how you hire, how you position, how you grow. Because you're no longer just competing on what you offer.

You're competing against what your community *has already built with you.*

In the final snippet of this chapter, we'll look at how this layered defensibility, trust, identity, and interdependence can be **intentionally reinforced over time**, without becoming rigid or cultish, because the most substantial moat is not a frozen wall.

It's a **living network** that learns how to hold itself.

Reinforcing the Moat Without Building a Fortress

One of the quiet dangers of a strong community is the temptation to overprotect it. As bonds deepen and rhythms set in, companies sometimes mistake fragility for value. They build walls where they should be planting trellises. They codify everything — norms, language, roles — until the very fluidity that made the community powerful starts to harden.

It comes from a good instinct: protect what's working. But community moats are not like castles. They don't need fortifications. They need **tending**. Barriers don't defend the strongest communities. They're sustained by *shared understanding* and enough space to evolve.

That's what makes a community durable: its ability to **retain coherence while absorbing change**.

And that ability can be nurtured but not forced.

The first way to reinforce a community moat without weakening it is to focus on **cultural memory**. Not policy. Not governance. Memory. Who remembers why the space was started? Who carries the stories of how early tensions were resolved? Who can point to the thread where a now-core ritual first emerged?

These aren't just sentimental details. They are **contextual infrastructure**. They shape how new members interpret what they see. They give shape to the invisible culture beneath the visible rules. And the more distributed that memory becomes, through artifacts, lore, replayed moments, the more stable the community feels, even as it grows.

You can support this without formal programs. A well-timed callback to a founding post. A regular "why we started" message in the onboarding flow. A quiet shoutout to a member who codified a key insight. These are not just acknowledgements. They are *anchors*. They keep the past lightly tethered to the present, just enough to keep the shape intact.

The second method is to design for **emergent leadership**. Instead of over-engineering moderation or centralizing authority, create paths for members to take responsibility in small, reversible ways. Let them run an event. Write a recap. Curate a resource. Then, slowly, widen that circle.

This reinforces the sense that the community isn't being held accountable for its members. They are keeping it.

And that feeling, of mutual holding, is the most potent form of defensibility. It means the system can flex without breaking. It means the brand is no longer the sole factor in maintaining trust. It's distributed. Shared. Internalized.

Finally, the long-term moat is secured not through control, but through **shared meaning**. The clearer the "why" of the community, the easier it is to let the "how" evolve. When members understand the essence of the space, the tone, the values, the shape of generosity, they can help maintain its integrity, even as formats shift, tools change, or people cycle in and out.

Meaning is what keeps a 10-year-old forum feeling alive. It's what allows a new Discord channel to gain traction in weeks. It's what makes a meetup more than just an event. When a community's meaning is legible, it doesn't need to be fragile. It can stretch.

And the more you allow that stretch, the more likely it is that your community won't just defend your company from churn, copycats, or irrelevance.

It will carry your brand into places you didn't predict.

That's the ultimate expression of a community moat, not a static structure, but a **living field** of mutual reinforcement, shaped by trust, guided by identity, protected not by restriction but by meaning.

In the next chapter, we'll pivot from defensibility to **differentiation**, exploring how communities don't just help companies survive but help them *stand apart* because the moat is only half the story.

The other half is the **strategic positioning** it enables.

PART II: DESIGNING A COMMUNITY-LED STRATEGY

Chapter 7: The Strategic Positioning Through Community

From Soft Signals to Strategic Advantage

Community is often talked about as a soft force, cultural, emotional, and ambient. It's seen as hard to measure, harder to predict, and even harder to "own." It's the stuff that happens between the product, around the brand, and beyond the roadmap. Leadership teams nod at its importance, then turn the conversation back to funnels, forecasts, and OKRs.

But something deeper is happening. Slowly, and then all at once, community is becoming **leverage**, not just for engagement or retention, but for **core strategy**. And the companies that realize this are quietly building unfair advantages. Not because their communities are bigger, but because they are designed to compound.

This chapter is about that turn: how the community moves from being a cultural layer to becoming a strategic engine. It doesn't just support what the business is doing, but **accelerates what it's trying to become**.

It begins with a mental shift: recognizing that communities are not audiences. They don't need to be "activated." They are already active. What they need is alignment between the energy of the people and the direction of the business.

When that alignment exists, the system begins to give back in surprising ways.

A product team gets faster feedback, not because they launched a survey, but because power users are already in conversation with each other. A marketing team reaches new audiences not through paid channels, but through shared trust, as members share ideas with peers who would never click an ad. A sales team sees conversion rise, not because of a new pitch deck, but because prospects already feel affinity, thanks to stories they've heard from inside the space.

None of this happens by accident. It occurs when a community becomes **strategically embedded**, not just as a brand wrapper, but as a force multiplier for the business itself.

I've seen this most clearly with companies that build what I'd call a **community-insight loop**. These are organizations that don't just host a forum or a Slack; they listen systematically. They observe what's being asked, what's being repeated, and what's starting to emerge. They feed those patterns back into their strategy: product, positioning, even hiring. And the result is not just faster iteration. It's a business that begins to mirror the needs and language of its community in real time.

One early-stage founder I worked with had been struggling with product-market fit. His tool was powerful but misunderstood. The positioning wasn't landing. The demo calls were clumsy. But buried in the community, particularly among early adopters, was a different way of describing the product. A metaphor that kept surfacing. A story that seemed to resonate more than anything the company had written.

He did something simple. He stopped writing copy and started collecting language. Community language. Forum replies. Long threads. Support DMs. He gathered what people were saying when they *loved* the product, not just when they used it. And from that language, a new pitch emerged, more precise, truer, closer to the real story.

Conversion jumped. But more importantly, so did confidence. His team now had a way to think about strategy not just from first principles, but from lived experience. The community wasn't a sounding board. It was an **insight surface**, always on, always reflecting, constantly shaping.

This is one form of strategic leverage. But it's not the only one.

In the next section, we'll explore how **community energy can be directed**, not controlled, but guided, to align with core business outcomes. Not just growth in size, but **depth in alignment**. Not just engagement metrics, but durable, compounding impact.

Because when a company learns to harness, not just host, its community, it doesn't just gain reach. It gains **resonance**.

Compounding Across Functions

Most departments work in silos, and by necessity. Product builds, marketing promotes, sales closes, support resolves. The handoffs are structured. The outputs are linear. Efficiency depends on clarity: who owns what, and when.

But communities don't behave like departments. They don't move linearly. They are porous, circular, and self-generating. And this is precisely why they can become such powerful sources of leverage, **because they move between domains**, pulling insight and energy from one function into another without formal permission.

When a community is healthy, marketing doesn't need to guess what language resonates. It can listen. Product doesn't need to create a new beta group for every iteration. Feedback is already flowing. Support doesn't need to chase down edge cases. The community has logged them. Even talent doesn't have to rely solely on recruiting campaigns. The next great hire might already be contributing on a forum or leading a discussion thread.

This is the compounding effect of community. The same signal, the same question, the same story, the same act of advocacy, can ripple across functions, touching five parts of the business before it even appears in a dashboard.

And because the system is human, not just technical, it doesn't just scale in size. It **deepens in usefulness**. Every contribution adds not just activity, but texture. Every shared experience becomes part of the company's ambient intelligence.

I've seen product teams shave months off their roadmap when community members build workarounds faster than engineering can. One company I supported had a quietly powerful community of power users, technically advanced, creatively impatient. They didn't wait for features. They built their own.

At first, the company saw this as a fringe case. "That's great for them," someone said in a roadmap meeting, "but our average user isn't doing that." Then someone else asked the better question: *What if these workarounds are the roadmap?* Not because they scale instantly, but because they signal where the product needs to go, what gaps are worth closing, and what workflows are worth integrating.

That shift in mindset unlocked an entirely new approach. Community contributions became not anecdotes, but **input streams**. The product team stopped framing the roadmap as a fixed plan and started treating it like a conversation, with the community as a co-author.

The effect wasn't chaos. It was **alignment**. A tighter loop between what people wanted, what they were building on their own, and what the company delivered.

The same dynamic plays out in marketing, but in reverse. While product pulls ideas from the community, marketing pushes stories back into it, not as scripts, but as signal amplifiers. The best community-led marketing doesn't broadcast at the edges. It listens at the core. It watches what people are already saying, and then sharpens it, echoes it, lifts it.

In one developer-focused brand, we noticed that the strongest referrals weren't coming from campaigns. They were coming from blog comments. Quiet acknowledgments in docs. A tweet that started, "Finally, someone built this…" The community didn't need to be asked to advocate. They were already doing it. What marketing needed to do was **document what was already working**, then feed it back into the system.

They began curating, not scripting, testimonials and highlighting use cases that emerged organically, creating microsites not for selling, but for surfacing community-built tools. The result? Higher authenticity. Lower cost. And a brand narrative that sounded like its users, because it *was* its users.

And perhaps most surprisingly, the leverage extended into areas the company hadn't planned for, including hiring, retention, and even **culture**.

When community spaces reflect the internal values of a company, they become magnets for aligned talent. Not because they were designed to recruit, but because they reveal something true. The best hires don't always apply through a careers page. Sometimes they start by answering a question, submitting a PR, and joining a discussion. A team lead spots the mindset, not just the resume. And a new kind of hiring begins, not just for skills, but for *fit*.

This is the quiet power of community-as-leverage. It moves sideways. It moves slowly. And then, all at once, it becomes indispensable.

In the next section, we'll look at how to design for **durability**, ensuring that this strategic advantage isn't fragile or overly dependent on a few core contributors, because leverage only matters if it lasts.

And in community systems, longevity doesn't come from volume. It comes from **coherence**.

Designing for Durability

It's easy to confuse activity with resilience. A Slack channel that lights up daily. Dozens of posts. Dozens more replies. Energy everywhere. But activity is not the same as durability. One is a snapshot. The other is a structure.

Durability in a community isn't defined by how much happens; it's defined by what **continues** when things get quiet, when leadership changes. When the product focus shifts. When team priorities pivot or pause. Strategic communities aren't just lively. They are **held** by systems, by culture, and increasingly, by each other.

What makes that possible isn't volume. It's coherence.

Coherence is what allows a community to retain its shape even as it grows, stretches, or adapts. It's the underlying clarity of why the space exists, who it's for, and how it works, not because those things are printed on a mission page, but because they are *lived*.

You can see coherence in small decisions: how conflict is handled, how newcomers are welcomed, how norms are maintained when no one's moderating. These are the decisions that define a community's center of gravity. And over time, they're what allow it to stay stable, even when everything else changes.

One executive once asked me, mid-consulting engagement, "How do we make sure this community doesn't just fall apart if our current lead leaves?" I told him the hard truth: *It will, if it depends on her.* Not because she's doing it wrong, but because she's doing too much. Her charisma, empathy, and responsiveness had built something beautiful. But beauty without structure is fragile.

So, we zoomed out. We mapped the interactions. Where was she filling in gaps that should be shared? Where had she become the only one holding certain rituals, answering key questions, defining tone?

Then we began slowly transferring those touchpoints, not all to new hires or more tooling, but to members themselves, not through mandates, but through mirrored ownership. When someone offered help, we invited them to shape more. When someone asked about norms, we shared not rules, but stories. The goal wasn't to formalize; it was to **distribute**.

Over the next few months, the leader stepped back slightly. And nothing broke. The space got stronger. Because what had looked like leadership was, in fact, a bottleneck. And once that bottleneck was cleared, the community began to breathe.

That's what it means to design for durability. You don't just build a system that works when it's well-staffed. You build a system that still works when it's lightly held.

And to do that, you need three things: **clarity**, **redundancy**, and **ritual**.

Clarity is the story the community tells about itself. Not just in theory, but in tone, in timing, in who gets heard and why. When people understand the community's purpose, they can effectively hold it together, even without explicit direction.

Redundancy is what protects against single points of failure. No one person holds all the context. No one tool carries all the weight. If a newsletter misses a week, the rhythm survives. If a moderator goes on leave, the culture persists because the system is **shared**.

And ritual is what gives time its shape. Recurring moments that anchor belonging: the Monday check-in, the monthly AMA, the quarterly retrospective. These aren't just events. They are **touchstones**, places where the community sees itself reflected, and renews its connection to the whole.

Most companies underestimate the importance of ritual. They treat it like content. But what ritual creates is **continuity**, not just between people, but across time. Ritual is what lets a new member feel part of something that existed before them, and what permits them to imagine themselves shaping it in the future.

These three design elements — clarity, redundancy, and ritual — don't require huge budgets or big platforms. They require attention. They require **letting go of control in favor of coherence**.

And when you do that, you get something rare: a community that doesn't collapse when it loses a leader. A system that continues to create value without needing constant inputs. A culture that evolves without drifting into incoherence.

You get leverage that lasts.

In the final section of this chapter, we'll look at how to align this kind of durability with **executive strategy**, so community isn't just an operational asset, but a leadership one, because the most effective community-led organizations don't treat community as an initiative. They treat it as **infrastructure**.

Community as Strategic Infrastructure

When a community sits at the edge of a company, tacked onto marketing, tethered to support, it behaves like a program. It follows the rules of campaigns: deadlines, deliverables, and outcomes. It asks, "What do we want our members to do this quarter?" It responds to strategy, but doesn't shape it.

But when community is centered, understood as a persistent system of insight, trust, and contribution, it begins to behave like **infrastructure**. Quiet. Foundational. Integral.

And that's when it starts shaping strategy from within.

The most evolved organizations I've worked with don't just run communities. They use the community as a **strategic listening device**. It's how they sense the market, test narratives. Anticipate needs. It's not just the front line of engagement; it's the **first layer of perception**.

In one mid-stage SaaS company, the executive team reviewed sales metrics, feature adoption, and support queues every Monday. But what shaped their big bets, how they framed customer problems, where they pointed the roadmap, wasn't any of those dashboards. It was the two hours they spent reading community threads, DMs, and live chat logs.

They weren't looking for noise. They were looking for **language**, the moments when users described a pain point with unusual clarity. Or praised something they didn't even know mattered. Or compared the product to a tool that the team had never considered a competitor. These were not product insights. They were **positioning insights**, evidence of how the market saw them, not how they saw themselves.

And this is what made their strategy sharper than their competitors'. They didn't just respond to the community. They **designed it**.

In another case, a founder told me that his best board meetings didn't revolve around metrics. They revolved around *stories* that his community surfaced. He would walk into the room not with slide decks, but with direct quotes from members: feedback loops, moments of advocacy, feature use in strange but brilliant ways. These weren't anecdotes. They were *indicators*. And over time, his investors came to trust those signals more than the spreadsheets.

This is what it looks like when community becomes part of how the company *thinks*.

It's easy to miss this leverage, because it doesn't shout. It doesn't come from sudden viral moments or massive events. It comes from the slow accumulation of trust, both within the company and externally. It comes from designing systems where members give because they feel seen. Where teams learn because they listen often. Where the distance between user and builder is short enough to feel like a conversation, not a transaction.

Most companies think strategy is about frameworks. But the best strategies don't just emerge from logic. They emerge from **pattern recognition**. From knowing not just what your users do, but what they *mean*. From sensing before the signal shows up in a KPI.

And no system reveals meaning more reliably, more humanely, more durably than a well-tended community.

That's why community matters at the executive level, not as a brand play, not as a support channel, but as a **strategic asset**. A surface area for learning. A container for feedback. A bridge to the edge of your market. A long-term multiplier of speed, clarity, and trust.

When leadership begins to see it this way, they stop asking "What do we get from the community?" and start asking, "What can we learn with it?" They stop funding it like a nice-to-have and start designing around it like a **core capability**.

And once that happens, the company doesn't just gain loyalty. It gains leverage that evolves with the world around it.

In the next chapter, we'll shift from the strategic to the operational, looking closely at the internal enablement required to support the community in practice because leverage isn't just an external effect. It's an internal commitment.

Chapter 8: Mapping Community to Business Goals

From Philosophy to Objectives

At some point in every community-led journey, someone in the room asks a very reasonable question:

"How does this tie back to the business?"

It's not a cynical question. It's a clarifying one. Because belief in community is not the same as alignment, you can believe in the value of connection, of trust, of member contribution, and still struggle to connect it to revenue, growth, or retention targets. You can have an inspired team, a vibrant forum, and still find yourself at a loss when the CFO asks what exactly it's contributing to the quarter.

This is where many community initiatives stall, not from lack of energy, but from lack of integration. The community sits adjacent to the business model, admired but not embedded. It becomes a kind of halo, emotionally powerful, but strategically ambiguous.

But when done right, community isn't a side project or a brand booster. It's a multiplier.

The key is specificity.

To make the community a strategic asset, you need to **tie it to objectives the business already tracks.** Do not invent new metrics. Do not bend your goals to fit someone else's dashboard. But meet the company where it is, then widen the lens.

I've seen this happen at companies of all sizes. A growth-stage SaaS platform reframed its ambassador program not as a "top of funnel play," but as a **distributed demand generation**

engine, producing leads that closed faster, with lower churn. A design tool used community-hosted events not as engagement moments, but as a **scalable sales assist**, warm environments where leads pre-qualified themselves before ever hitting a pipeline. A consumer health app discovered that its most valuable cohort, measured by LTV, was almost entirely composed of members who'd contributed to a shared challenge, forum, or review.

In all these cases, the community wasn't doing something *extra* for the business. It was doing something **essential**, just through different mechanics.

So, the question becomes: how do you map those mechanics?

How do you draw a clear line between what the community creates and what the business needs?

It starts with understanding that community is not a department, it's a set of distributed levers.

Levers that affect sales velocity, product velocity, customer lifetime value, recruiting efficiency, and brand affinity. But you don't see those levers unless you're looking through the right lens. And most teams aren't trained to look. They see community as engagement. They count posts, likes, and attendance. Not referrals. Not roadmap input. Not dealing with acceleration. Not cultural stickiness that leads to lower employee turnover.

The first step is shifting the frame from **channel to contribution**.

Instead of asking "How active is our community?" ask:
- ➤ "How many leads originated from community interaction?"
- ➤ "What percent of roadmap feedback came from trusted contributors?"

> ➢ "How much peer-to-peer support reduced help desk tickets?"
> ➢ "Which hires came in through community paths?"
> ➢ "How has retention differed between engaged members and passive users?"

These aren't soft signals. These are **business drivers**, just hiding in relational wrapping.

In the next section, we'll walk through each domain — **growth, product, success, and talent** — and look at how to build connective tissue between your community strategy and the goals your stakeholders already care about.

Because the power of community isn't just that it creates value, it's that it makes the kind of value every team is already chasing.

Revenue: Community as a Growth Engine

For all the high-minded talk of belonging, trust, and participation, most companies still live and die by the same reality: **revenue must grow**. No matter how visionary the strategy or thoughtful the values, business health is measured, at least in part, by dollars earned and customers gained.

The mistake isn't in measuring revenue. The mistake is in assuming that the community can't contribute to it in structured, strategic ways.

In truth, community is one of the most powerful revenue levers available to a company, if you know where to look.

The most obvious path is **lead generation, not** in the cold, transactional sense of "capturing emails" or "funneling traffic," but in the warm, compounding sense of *attraction*. When someone participates in a thriving, member-driven space, whether it's a Discord server, a subreddit, or a conference booth with actual community energy, they're not just exposed to a product. They're *immersed in a culture*. And culture is much harder to walk away from than copy.

I've watched this happen over and over. A design leader attends a live critique circle run by community members, not employees: no hard sell, no CTAs, just honest feedback on real work. Two weeks later, her team signed a six-figure contract, not because the session was a pitch, but because the **community framed the brand as trustworthy, expert, and real**. The product was just a layer in the experience.

That's not content marketing. That's **context marketing**, value that emerges from relevance and presence, not production.

But beyond leads, community accelerates **conversion**. Especially in high-consideration environments like B2B SaaS, buyers need more than a landing page. They need confidence. They need social proof that feels unfiltered. They need a way to explore the culture they're about to buy into.

And nothing does that better than a healthy, visible, participatory community.

Think of a prospective customer lurking in a public Slack space or attending a user group event. They're watching how people talk, how they're supported. What's the vibe?. They're not just evaluating features. They're assessing *their feelings*. Does this seem like a space I want to be in? Will I be ignored or uplifted? Will I be just another user, or a co-creator?

Every time they see someone answer a question thoughtfully, every time a community host tags a newcomer and makes them feel seen, every time a member shares something clever they built on your stack, they're getting **buy-in not** just to your tool, but to your ecosystem. And that ecosystem can become your single greatest asset in converting skeptics into champions.

One founder once told me, "We stopped thinking of the sales funnel as a sequence. We started thinking of it as a community gradient." Cold leads don't need nurturing. They need **to be invited**. Warm leads don't need closing. They need *belonging*. And community, when structured right, handles both.

Even more interesting is the community's role in **expansion**.

In subscription-based businesses, net revenue retention is gold. It's not just about keeping customers; it's about growing them. Community supports that in three key ways:

1. When new features are shared and celebrated in the community, they travel faster and with more legitimacy.

2. In B2B, users are often siloed. A strong community bridges roles. Product users influence finance buyers. Admins influence procurement.

3. When customers see how others are succeeding, through templates, shared outcomes, and showcases, they expand usage. Not because you pitched them, but because the community proved it.

These outcomes don't require manipulation or hard sales. They require **design**. You need to structure spaces where contributions are visible, new use cases emerge, and peers help each other imagine more ambitious outcomes.

When that happens, your community becomes not just a support layer. Not just a marketing layer. But a **sales engine** that grows more powerful with every new member it activates.

In the next section, we'll shift to **retention and customer success**, where the community's impact is subtler, but just as measurable, because keeping customers isn't just about solving problems.

It's about helping people feel less alone in the journey.

Retention: The Emotional Infrastructure of Loyalty

Customer success is often framed as a logistics problem. If people know how to use the product, they'll stay. If they're supported when things go wrong, they won't churn. But retention, at its core, isn't just about access to resources or speed of support. It's about how a person feels **after the first wave of novelty wears off.**

Do they still feel seen? Do they feel part of something in motion? Do they believe they're progressing, not just in skill, but in identity?

This is where community plays a quiet, decisive role, not as a replacement for successful teams or help docs, but as an emotional infrastructure that holds people in place **after the excitement fades.**

In traditional models, a customer buys the product and is then handed off to a success manager, or dropped into a tutorial flow, or left to navigate a help center. The logic is sound: equip, onboard, support. But what's missing is any sense of **continuity.** The customer may become more competent, but they don't become more **connected.** And when frustration eventually arrives, and it always does, they don't have enough relational tether to hold them in.

Community solves this by filling in the relational gaps. When someone has a question and gets a thoughtful reply, not just from a support agent, but from a peer, they're not just getting help.

They're getting **affirmation** that they matter. When they share something small they learned, and someone else builds on it, they're not just contributing content. They're being **reflected**. These are not soft feelings. These are the anchors of long-term retention.

I've seen this most clearly in developer communities. A platform can provide all the technical documents in the world, but what keeps users engaged isn't just documentation. It's **co-presence**, the knowledge that someone else has been where they are and is willing to share the path. That doesn't show up in a dashboard, but it shows up in behavior. Customers who participate in a community space, even once, are dramatically more likely to stick around. Not because they found the answer, but because they saw the room.

And that room, when well held, becomes the place people return to *before* they consider canceling. It becomes a space of recommitment. When someone's feeling stuck and sees others still building, iterating, and excited, they're more likely to give the product another try, not because of a feature update. But because of a **social signal**: you're not alone.

This is especially critical in products with long activation cycles, tools that take time to master, and workflows that require habit formation. In those cases, traditional success metrics often lag reality. A user may be on the edge of a breakthrough, or the edge of churn, and you won't see it in usage stats. But in a community, you see it **in conversation**. You hear it in how they talk. You catch it in what they post, or don't.

That's why some of the most innovative companies I've worked with don't treat community as a bonus layer. They treat it as a **listening device**. They track tone as closely as tickets. They don't just tag product bugs; they flag emotional friction. They design rituals that keep people moving forward. And they measure not just participation, but **trajectory**: is this person deepening? Are they becoming more confident, more expressive, more influential?

Because the clearest signal of retention isn't login frequency, it's **identity formation**.

When a customer starts using phrases the community coined, when they begin welcoming newcomers, when they refer to the product as "our stack" instead of "your tool", you've crossed a threshold. They're no longer just a user. They're a **member**. And members don't churn easily.

In the next section, we'll move beyond customers and toward the **product itself**, exploring how community doesn't just support usage, but shapes what gets built, what gets prioritized, and how innovation is sustained.

Because the most profound loyalty comes not from being supported...

...but from being **heard**.

Product: Co-Creation at Scale

Every company claims to prioritize building with the customer in mind. But for most, that means little more than an upvote board, a quarterly survey, or a handful of support tickets triaged into a product backlog. The truth is that most feedback loops are **performative**. They create the impression of listening, but not the experience of being heard.

A strategic community flips that model. It doesn't treat customers as data points. It treats them as **co-authors**.

In a mature community, product ideas don't just trickle in from the sidelines. They **emerge organically** through lived use, edge cases, and workarounds. You don't have to ask for feedback, because it's already happening, in posts, conversations, shared artifacts. And it's far more nuanced than a poll of roadmaps. It's contextual. It's tested. It's emotionally loaded with what customers *care about*.

This kind of ambient product insight is gold. But most companies miss it, not because they don't value it, but because they're not structurally set up to receive it. The product team and the community team are separated. Insights are gathered informally. There's no loop. No rhythm. Just fragments.

But when you operationalize that connection, everything changes.

I remember working with a company that made creative software. Their community was full of power users who were constantly inventing new use cases, hacks, plugins, and workflows that stretched the product beyond its intended design. At first, the product team saw it as noise. Too specific. Too weird. But eventually they realized these weren't edge cases. They were *future cases*. Signals of what the most invested users needed before the rest of the market even knew to ask for it.

Once they started routing those insights properly, weekly synthesis, shared Slack channels, and internal tagging conventions, the roadmap began to change. Features were shipped faster. Messaging improved. Adoption rates rose. Not because they were moving faster, but because they were moving **with greater fidelity** to what people wanted.

The community didn't slow the product down with more opinions. It **sped it up** by reducing guesswork.

But the real magic happens when you go one step further, when community members aren't just the source of feedback, but the **co-creators of value**.

That might look like inviting contributors to prototype tools. It might mean letting trusted members into private betas, not just for testing, but for shaping. It might mean sourcing templates, guides, components, or creative assets directly from the people who live closest to the product's edge.

When you do that, product development stops being a linear process and starts to look like an **ecosystem**. Some ideas come from inside. Others rise from the ground. The company doesn't just ship features. It **curates momentum**.

And the benefit isn't just velocity. It's *resonance*. When features are born from within the community, their adoption is immediate. Early champions are already in place. Use cases are already documented. The story tells itself, because it was written together.

This is the kind of product loop that no competitor can mimic overnight. Because it doesn't live in dashboards, it lives in **trust**.

In the next section, we'll explore how community strategy links to **talent and hiring**, a goal often overlooked but increasingly essential. Because in a world where talent moves fast, the most substantial recruiting moat isn't compensation or perks. It's belonging before the first interview.

Hiring and Culture: The Talent Moat

Recruiting is a trust game. You can have the perfect role, the best comp package, the shiniest brand, but if a candidate doesn't trust what it feels like to work with you, they'll hesitate. And in the long arc of a hiring market, that hesitation is costly. It adds friction, slows cycles, and raises your hiring CAC just as surely as it does in sales.

What the community offers is more than just a funnel of interested applicants. It offers **proof-of-culture.**

When a company's values are only visible on the careers page, they read like aspirations. When they're visible in a living community, embedded in how people speak, how they support each other, how disagreement is handled, they become **evidence.** And the evidence is robust.

I've seen this most clearly in product-led companies where the community and the team often overlap. A candidate doesn't just hear that the company values design, or curiosity, or generosity; they **see it** in how the community operates. They watch team members show up consistently, not just to lead, but to listen. They witness rituals that prioritize recognition, inclusion, and transparency. And somewhere in that quiet observation, the narrative begins to shift.

The company stops being a brand. It starts becoming a **place.**

That sense of place is often what pulls in the highest quality talent, not because it's flashy, but because it's *real.* A product manager notices that the way roadmap feedback is handled in public matches the way cross-functional teams operate internally. A developer sees how moderators handle conflict in the forums and imagines what engineering standups might feel like. A marketer considers the tone of newsletters and community responses, understanding that tone isn't just performance; it's a cultural baseline.

Community becomes a kind of **pre-onboarding**. A way for future teammates to rehearse alignment before a job post even goes live.

And the loop continues after hire. Employees who came through the community are often **higher-trust, faster-integrating, and more value-aligned**. They don't just bring skills. They get shared context. They've absorbed the rhythms, the norms, the shorthand. They don't need to be taught the culture, because they've already been *part of it*.

In early-stage companies, this can be a competitive edge. In larger orgs, it becomes a retention tool. Because culture isn't something you impose. It's something you **reinforce through presence**. When the community is active and aligned, it keeps that presence alive, even as teams grow, restructure, and evolve.

The same applies to external collaborators, freelancers, contractors, and advisors. A community-led ecosystem makes it easy to tap talent without friction. Need a workshop facilitator? A content strategist? A localization expert? In a vibrant community, the "bench" isn't hidden. It's **already visible**. Reputation lives in the open.

And that visibility creates both efficiency and accountability. When people work in the open, with their community identity at stake, they show up differently. There's more pride. More continuity. More shared sense of momentum.

So, when someone asks how community connects to hiring, you can answer plainly: it's not just a pipeline.

It's **cultural infrastructure**. It's where your next best teammate is already watching, already learning, deciding if they want to be part of what you're building.

And they're not just watching what you post. They're watching how the *community behaves when you're not in the room.*

That behavior becomes your employer brand, whether you control it or not.

And if the behavior is generous, innovative, dynamic, and human, then the brand will be too.

In the next chapter, we'll finally put numbers to this story. Because even the most powerful community strategy needs **metrics that matter**, numbers that tell the truth, signal progress, and reinforce that this isn't a side project. It's the **core business strategy**.

Chapter 9: Community Metrics That Matter

Measuring What Moves the Needle

Sooner or later, every community leader faces the exact moment: a slide deck, a board meeting, a skeptical executive across the table. And the question lands, sometimes softly, sometimes like a hammer:

"Can you prove this is working?"

It's not an unfair question. It's the right one. Because community, for all its energy and story-rich charm, still lives inside businesses that run on metrics. And metrics don't care how inspiring your member story is. They care whether the effort is *moving the industry forward.*

But here's the trap: when community leaders try to answer that question, they often reach for the easiest signals. Growth in Discord members. Retweets on an event post. Number of signups to a monthly newsletter. These are visible. Easy to track. They look good on slides.

And they're almost always **vanity metrics**.

Because while they signal activity, they don't tell you whether anything meaningful is happening. They don't tell you whether trust is being built. Whether knowledge is compounding. Whether members are becoming contributors or just passing through, we're interested in their experiences.

Real community metrics aren't about reach. They're about **depth**.

And to measure depth, you need to know what kind of system you're operating. Community is not a funnel. It's a **network**. It doesn't follow the logic of conversion. It follows the logic of **connection**.

That means our metrics need to shift, too.

In a funnel, you ask: how many entered? How many moved forward? How many converted?

In a community, you ask: who's connected? How strong are the ties? How often do they return? What kinds of value are being exchanged, and by whom?

This kind of measurement isn't always simple. It requires interpretation. But it also opens the door to far more **insightful storytelling**, the kind that helps executives see what's happening beneath the surface.

I recall a team that had expanded its forum to 10,000 members. Everyone celebrated, a significant number. Clear progress. But when they looked closer, 94% of posts came from just 3% of members. Of those, most were asking questions, and only a small handful were answering. When they dug deeper still, they found the real community, the *trusted core*, was less than 50 people. And those 50 were responsible for almost every answer, template, event, and signal of life.

The significant number had told one story. The small number said the truth.

And the truth was powerful, because it gave the team something to protect, something to nurture. Instead of chasing the next 10,000, they began designing for their **core contributors**. And from there, the real growth began.

In the next section, we'll explore what those "core metrics" actually look like, not in isolation, but in context, because community health isn't a single number. It's a **constellation of**

behaviors, each one pointing toward a deeper story of trust, participation, and shared ownership.

Because in the end, what you measure is what you invite.

And if you want a deep, resilient, impactful community, you need to measure more than attendance. You need to measure **aliveness**.

Signals of Aliveness: What to Look For

The most valuable signals in a community often don't show up on the dashboard. They appear in the spaces between events. In the pauses between replies. In the moments when no one's watching, someone always is.

That's the strange paradox of community work: the things that matter most are often the least measurable by default. And yet, once you learn what to listen for, a kind of map begins to emerge.

One of the first signals worth tuning into is **depth of engagement**. Not how many people clicked into a thread. But how long did they stay? What they said. Whether their reply showed understanding or just repetition, a single thoughtful post from someone who reflects on another member's idea, builds on it, and contributes a perspective rooted in lived experience, that's worth more than 50 emoji reacts.

Depth reveals intent. And intent, when it shows up consistently, turns into trust.

You can sense this when members begin referencing each other's contributions, when language loops back on itself. When someone says, "As Alex shared last week…" or "This builds on the framework we made in that event…" That kind of contextual weaving is more than social nicety. It's a **sign of memory**. And memory is what makes a group into a culture.

The second powerful signal is **activation velocity**, not just how many people join, but how quickly they move from observer to participant. Every community has a gravitational threshold: the moment when a newcomer decides whether they're just browsing or truly joining. Measuring the time between sign-up and first meaningful action, such as posting, commenting, or attending, can tell you everything about how welcoming your space is.

In fast-moving communities, activation often happens within hours. Someone joins, is greeted, and participates the same day. In slower systems, it might take weeks. The point isn't to enforce urgency, but to observe **where the friction is hiding**. Are expectations unclear? Are the social cues too subtle? Are early experiences rewarding or flat?

The most successful community-led companies I've worked with don't just celebrate new sign-ups. They celebrate new contributors. And they measure how many cross that line, and how many stay there.

Which brings us to contribution patterns.

Contribution is where a community's energy shifts from passive to generative. It's the moment someone decides not just to consume value, but to create it. And that moment can look many ways: a comment, a shared resource, a volunteer gesture, a spontaneous welcome to someone new.

The question to ask isn't just "who is contributing?" but "how often do contributions recur, and from how broad a base?"

A community with ten prolific posters and 2,000 silent readers might look active. But it's brittle. Lose one of those ten, and the scaffolding trembles. By contrast, a community with 300 contributors, each offering small but regular input, is **dense**. It's networked. It's stable in motion.

That density is what matters.

It tells you that contribution isn't heroic, it's **normalized**. And when the contribution is normalized, the scale becomes safe.

Finally, we come to **relational stickiness**, the most complex signal to quantify, but perhaps the most strategic.

You can start to see it in recurring names. In mutual replies. In moments of casual familiarity. A joke lands because it references last month. A concern is raised and gently de-escalated, not by staff, but by another member who's earned quiet authority. These aren't statistics. They're **stories that signal structure**. They show you that the social web is holding, not just through policy, but through presence.

These are the signs of aliveness. Not vanity numbers. Not performance dashboards. But **evidence that a culture is forming**, that meaning is circulating, that the weight of the community is being shared.

And while some of these things can be approximated by metrics, such as DAUs, thread length, and repeat contributors, the real work is interpretive. You don't just analyze these signals. You **listen to them**.

Because they don't just tell you what happened, they tell you what's *about to happen*.

In the next section, we'll look at how to build a metrics framework that blends these human signals with operational ones, enough to satisfy stakeholders, without sacrificing the soul of the space.

Because a truly alive community can be measured, you have to **look where the numbers can't point on their own.**

Designing a Metrics Framework That Doesn't Kill the Spirit

Metrics should clarify, not flatten. But too often, in the rush to make community legible to the business, we try to compress something fluid and relational into a set of static numbers. We turn a living system into a scorecard. And in doing so, we risk erasing exactly what makes it powerful.

The goal isn't to resist measurement. The goal is to design measurements that reveal **meaning without reducing it**. That starts with a simple but often overlooked shift: measuring *from the inside out*, not the outside in.

Most community dashboards are built backwards. They begin with stakeholder questions, such as how many members? How much activity? How much growth? And then scramble to retrofit answers from platform data. This leads to reporting that feels disconnected, hollow, and worse, misaligned with what matters to members.

But what if you flipped the order?

What if you started with community behavior — actual moments of connection, contribution, insight — and then translated *those* into signals the business could understand?

That's how a good framework works. It's not just a report. It's a **bridge**. It connects the nuance of community life to the imperatives of business growth. Without distortion. Without dilution.

Start by anchoring your framework in **purpose**. What is this community here to do? Is it meant to reduce the support burden? Fuel product feedback? Deepen brand affinity? Not all goals are equal, and not every community serves the same ones. You don't need fifty metrics. You need **clarity**.

If your community's purpose is to power product innovation, then your most important metric isn't DAU. It's the velocity and quality of actionable feedback. If the goal is to increase retention, then focus on re-engagement rates and relational depth. If the purpose is talent discovery, then you measure hiring conversion from community referrals, not likes on a hiring post.

Every metric you choose should pass a simple test: Does this help us understand whether the community is fulfilling its strategic function? If not, it's noise.

Once you've defined purpose, the next step is to categorize signals into three transparent layers: **participation**, **contribution**, and **outcome**.

Participation tells you who's showing up. It's foundational, but not sufficient. Contribution tells you who's adding value. It's the heartbeat. Outcome tells you what changes because of that value, inside the business, inside the member, or both. It's the evidence that the system works.

And you need all three.

A community with high participation but low contribution is shallow. A community with high contribution but no measurable outcomes is self-contained. The best communities balance all three: visible motion, meaningful creation, and shared return.

But perhaps the most overlooked part of a metrics framework is **interpretation**.

Raw numbers are meaningless unless someone is there to read them **in context**.

This is why so many community reports fail to land. They present stats without a story. "We had 400 attendees." "We saw

18% more posts." But they never say what that means. They never explain why it matters or what decisions it should inform.

Strong community operators don't just count. They narrate. They add human texture to quantitative signals. They point to a surge in replies, explaining that it came from a conflict and how it was resolved. They track a dip in attendance and connect it to a product delay, or a moment of trust broken and later repaired. They don't just report what happened. They **interpret what it means**.

In community settings, the most important metrics are often **leading indicators**, not lagging ones. You see signals of momentum, or fatigue, weeks before they show up in churn or NPS. But only if you're looking with the right frame.

In the final section of this chapter, we'll examine how to **communicate community metrics upward**, so that executives and stakeholders don't just tolerate your reports but begin to see them as vital signals for the business.

Because when you measure the right things and tell the right story, community stops being an anecdotal asset. It becomes a **strategic dashboard** of its own.

Translating Community to the Boardroom

You can have the richest engagement, the strongest contribution loops, the healthiest sense of belonging, and still lose influence if you can't explain it in the room where decisions are made. Not because executives don't care. But because they live in a world of ratios, deltas, and forecasts. And unless the community can be seen through that lens, it stays on the edge of the strategy table, admired but rarely resourced.

The challenge, and the opportunity, is to tell the **truth of the community** in a language that lets it move.

That doesn't mean stripping out the soul. It means structuring the story.

When you walk into an executive meeting, you're not just representing sentiment. You're representing **signals of the future state**. What's shifting in your member base? What behaviors are emerging that might predict churn, upsell, adoption, or risk? How is community revealing what quantitative dashboards won't see until it's too late?

The most effective community leaders are translators. They take the language of belonging, reciprocity, and trust, and they turn it into **operational insight**. A story of growing contributor diversity becomes a signal of reduced dependency on customer support. An uptick in high-signal questions reveals not just interest, but product-market misalignment, or opportunity. A drop in return participation after a major release may surface an onboarding gap before support tickets spike.

In other words, community is early intelligence.

But that intelligence has to be framed in motion. Executives respond to narrative movement: up, down, forward, blocked. So when reporting community health, structure the story like a forecast. What's trending? What's changing? What's at risk, and what's ripening?

And always bring it back to **consequence**.

If the community's contributor core is shrinking, what happens to peer support capacity? If newcomer engagement is accelerating, what does that suggest about product onboarding? If events are seeing more spontaneous member-led sessions, what does that signal about advocacy potential?

The best reports don't just inform. They create **shared urgency**.

They move leaders from passive observation to active support. They invite investment, not by pleading, but by **showing the community's relevance to core business outcomes**. Revenue. Retention. Reputation. Roadmap. Recruitment.

Not every executive will speak to the community." But every executive speaks of **risk and return**.

So frame your insights through that dual lens. Show what the business gains by supporting this layer of human infrastructure, and what it risks by neglecting it.

Because in a market increasingly shaped by trust, affinity, and word-of-mouth, community isn't just a strategic lever. It's a **strategic listening system**.

And those who know how to listen and report what they hear will always have a seat at the table.

In the next chapter, we'll examine what it takes to **govern a community well**, not just in metrics, but in ownership, roles, and accountability. When the system is working, the next question becomes "Is this valuable?" It's "Who holds the keys?"

Chapter 10: Governance, Roles, and Ownership

The Quiet Question at the Heart of Every Community

Every thriving community, at some point, runs into the same invisible wall. Growth is happening. Participation is strong. Members are engaged. But beneath the surface, something begins to fray, not in the culture, but in the clarity. Who is responsible for what? Who has the authority to make a change? Who decides when enough is enough?

The questions don't erupt all at once. They surface quietly, and often in moments of stress. A conflict escalates, and no one's sure who should step in. A new feature rolls out, and it's unclear if the moderators were informed. A passionate contributor feels ignored, leaving the core team uncertain about how to respond.

This isn't failure. Its **emergence**. A signal that the system has grown from instinct to infrastructure. What used to run on vibes now needs structure. Not bureaucracy. Not corporate stiffness. Just enough **governance** to sustain the trust that made the community thrive in the first place.

But governance is a tricky word. It carries a shadow. People hear it and brace for rules, rigidity, and red tape. The fear is real: that too much structure will kill the magic. That turning something organic into something operational will strip it of the very thing that made it work.

And that fear is justified, because governance, applied too early or too bluntly, *can* collapse a community's momentum. But no governance at all leads to something just as dangerous: **burnout, bottlenecks, and hidden hierarchies**.

What we need instead is a more fluid definition. Governance is not about control, but rather a **container**. Not a system that tells people what they can't do, but one that clarifies how we move together when things get complex.

Because complexity is coming, if it's not already here.

The real art is to build governance that's strong enough to hold growth, but light enough to remain flexible. A structure that adapts as the community evolves. A set of roles and norms that are not fixed in concrete, but etched in sand, visible, meaningful, but open to redrawing.

In newer communities, this might start with questions of moderation. Who enforces guidelines? Who gets flagged in moments of confusion or tension? But as the system matures, those questions expand: Who stewards the roadmap for community evolution? Who holds the rituals? Who brings new contributors into leadership?

At its best, governance becomes a shared choreography. Not everyone is dancing the same steps, but everyone understands the rhythm and knows where to turn, when to lead, and when to yield. And like any good choreography, it requires **clear roles**.

That's what we'll begin exploring in the next section: how to define, assign, and evolve roles in a way that protects energy, scales contribution, and avoids the trap of founder-dependence or team bottlenecks.

Because if the community is to become a **core operating layer**, it needs more than enthusiasm. It requires shared responsibility, clearly held.

From Chaos to Clarity: The Role Spectrum

In the early days of a community, roles tend to emerge informally. Someone naturally takes the lead on welcoming new members. Someone else starts curating resources. Another becomes the quiet center of gravity that others begin to orbit. These roles are rarely discussed. They form, like rocks in a riverbed, shaped by flow, not by plan.

This is both beautiful and fragile.

When roles are unspoken, they rely on continuity. The person who shows up keeps showing up. Until they don't. And when that happens, when someone quietly steps back, or burns out, or leaves without fanfare, the absence is deeply felt but often misunderstood. It feels like something *broke* when, in reality, the system lacked **clarity**.

So, the shift to intentional roles is less about hierarchy and more about **honoring energy**. It says: This work matters. Let's name it. Let's support it. Let's make it sustainable, so that it doesn't rest on invisible labor or quiet obligation.

Every community eventually needs this shift. But the way it's done matters.

The most effective communities don't start by listing tasks. They begin by naming **postures**. Ways of showing up. A core team that stewards direction. A circle of facilitators who hold space. A web of contributors who respond, share, build, and host. These are not job titles. They function in a living system. And each one carries a different rhythm, a different weight, a different form of accountability.

The core team, in most cases, holds the frame. They steward vision, maintain alignment with the broader business, and ensure resources are flowing. They don't control every thread, but they understand the shape of the whole. They are stewards more than owners.

Moderators and facilitators often operate closer to the ground. They guide the tone. They enforce community guidelines, not with harshness, but with consistency and care. Their job is to make the implicit explicit. To keep the soil healthy so others can grow.

Then there are the contributors. Often, the most under-recognized and essential layer is the one that matters most. These are the people who host the event, write the blog post, answer the forum question, and start the new ritual. They don't hold structural power, but they have **cultural power**, and over time, that power defines the very texture of the space.

As a community matures, these roles evolve. Some contributors step into stewardship. Some stewards step back into participation. Some newcomers rise quickly into trusted leadership, not because of tenure, but because of alignment and presence.

And that's the key: roles must be **porous**.

Too often, companies formalize roles too tightly. They assign badges, titles, tiers, and suddenly a living network begins to ossify. People feel locked in or locked out. Contribution becomes permissioned. Emergence slows.

But when roles are fluid, when people can move between them with light structure and clear support, communities gain both stability and adaptability. They're not just resilient. They're **alive**.

This requires more than naming. It requires a light scaffolding of **expectations and transitions**. What does it mean to step into a role? How is support provided? How does someone step out with grace, without guilt? When these questions are answered openly, people feel safe to show up **as they are**, without fear of overcommitment or confusion.

In the next section, we'll explore how **ownership** works, not just of tasks, but of direction, identity, and even conflict. Because as roles take shape, so too must the questions of **authority and accountability**.

And in the community, those questions are never just operational. They're **relational by nature**.

The Shape of Shared Ownership

Ownership in the community isn't just about responsibilities. It's about relationship, to the group, to the mission, to the identity of the space itself. And because of that, ownership is never purely operational. It's **emotional**. It's charged. And it's often ambiguous until it's tested.

Most communities begin with implicit ownership. The founders, the hosts, and the core team set the tone, hold the center, and make the calls. It works for a while. But as the community grows, what once felt clear begins to blur. Members step forward with ideas. Contributors ask for more input. Leaders start to feel pressure to say yes to everything, or worse, to disappear behind a wall of indecision.

That's when the cracks start to show. Not because anyone is doing anything wrong, but because the **system hasn't clarified its boundaries**.

Who decides what gets built? Who owns the vision? Can a long-time member propose a structural change? If so, how is that decision made? If not, why not? And who gets to say?

Without answers to these questions, even the strongest communities begin to falter, not from lack of energy, but from the friction of misaligned expectations.

Shared ownership doesn't mean shared decision-making on everything. It doesn't mean consensus. It means **clarity of the domain**. It means defining what's open for participation, what's open for feedback, and what remains centralized for good reason.

In a healthy system, different layers of ownership coexist. The core team might own the long-term vision. The contributors might own programs, events, or specific rituals. The broader member base owns the tone, the momentum, and the cultural memory. And each of these layers needs to be named, not rigidly, but with enough signal that no one has to guess where they stand.

That signal can come in the form of charters, working groups, open calls for proposals, or even lightweight agreements. What matters isn't the format. It's the **presence of a social contract**, a shared understanding of who holds what, and how that holding can evolve.

Without this, resentment builds. When contributors feel they're doing meaningful work but lack influence, they drift, or worse, they disengage silently. When core teams feel overwhelmed by invisible expectations, they start withdrawing. The trust that made the community flourish begins to calcify into **tension no one wants to name**.

But when ownership is distributed with care, something powerful happens. People stop waiting for permission. They start proposing, iterating, and leading. Not because they were told to, but because the structure **invited it**.

That invitation is what makes governance humane. It says, "This is not ours alone." It's ours to hold together, differently, at different times, in ways that respect both autonomy and alignment.

Of course, shared ownership doesn't eliminate conflict. It often surfaces more of it. But it also gives the tools to navigate that conflict, because people understand where responsibility lies, and where the edges of that responsibility are. They're not just reacting. They're **responding with shared context**.

And when someone steps out of a role or hands off a project, the clarity of ownership means the momentum doesn't die with them. It continues because the community is aware of how the system works. Because it was designed to be **bigger than any one person**.

In the next and final section of this chapter, we'll look at how governance can evolve without ossifying. Because strategy needs structure, but structure, without reflection, can become a cage.

And community was never meant to be caged.

Living Systems Need Living Structure

All structures decay unless they are refreshed. That's true in organizations, and it's doubly true in communities, because the very thing you're governing is not static. It's made of people. And people change. They grow, they drift, they deepen, they leave. If the structures around them don't change, too, they stop fitting. And when structure stops fitting, it starts constraining.

That's why community governance isn't something you set and forget. It's something you **steward**, a system of agreements that remains in motion, even as the community itself matures.

The mistake many teams make is assuming that structure must be finalized. That at some point, the governance model will be "done." But that's not how living systems work. They don't freeze. They **pulse**. They respond. They stretch and tighten. They adjust as new needs emerge and old ones fade.

The communities that last are the ones that **bake adaptation into their design**.

This can take many forms. Some communities hold regular governance retros, not to critique, but to reflect: What's still working? What feels heavy? Where are decisions getting stuck? Others rotate roles intentionally, letting members cycle through positions of leadership to prevent bottlenecks and keep perspective fresh. Some create temporary roles, projects with a start and end point, so responsibility doesn't default into permanence.

What matters is that the system stays **conscious of itself**.

When governance is alive, it becomes not just a set of rules, but a way of **paying attention**. You begin to notice when a role has outlived its purpose. When a ritual no longer serves the group, it becomes outdated, and when someone has become a quiet center of leadership but isn't recognized. These observations aren't threats. They're **data**. And if the structure has enough give, that data turns into action.

A healthy governance system also creates room for **emergent voices**. It doesn't just reinforce existing hierarchies; it stays open to new patterns of leadership. Someone who consistently shows up, builds trust, and demonstrates care should have a path toward deeper responsibility, even if they weren't in the founding circle. If the structure makes it impossible for new energy to rise, the community will stagnate. Not immediately. But eventually. Every time.

That's why reflection isn't optional. It's the only way to avoid **structural inertia**, the slow creep of "this is how we've always done it," even when no one remembers why.

Governance, at its best, is a kind of group memory. It holds what matters, so that no one person has to. But it must also be willing to forget, to release what's no longer serving. To allow space for new rituals, new roles, new rhythms.

That doesn't mean chaos. It means **dynamic stability**. A structure that bends without breaking. A team that evolves without losing the thread. A space that grows without growing apart.

So, as your community expands, across products, across cultures, across time zones, ask not just what should be held, but **how**. Ask not just who leads, but who might, if given a chance. Ask not just what is working now, but what might need to end, to make room for what's next.

Because governance isn't about power, it's about care, distributed wisely. And care, like any form of energy, needs **movement to stay alive**.

In the next chapter, we turn from structure to creativity. From roles and rules to innovation. We'll explore what happens when your community stops being a support layer...

...and becomes a driver of the product itself.

Chapter 11: Community-Led Product Development

When Product Becomes a Conversation

In most companies, product development is a cycle of prediction. Research. Hypothesis. Prioritization. Build. Ship. Hope. Feedback comes in, mainly after the fact. If it's good, the team breathes. If it's bad, they pivot. The process is efficient, even elegant. But it's also brittle, because the distance between builder and user is still too vast.

That's where community changes everything.

When you build a relationship with your users, not just for them, you collapse that distance. You start to see the product not as a set of features, but as a **shared language**. Something everyone is shaping, even if they never write a line of code.

This shift doesn't happen automatically. It begins when teams stop treating the community as a post-launch feedback loop and start treating it as a **real-time design surface**. A place where ideas are floated, tested, broken, and rebuilt, *before* they're formalized. A space where usage becomes dialogue, not a data point.

I recall a small dev tool startup that pivoted its entire onboarding sequence, not due to an A/B test, but because a member in their forum explained, step by step, where they got lost and why. The explanation wasn't angry. It was thoughtful, generous, precise. And because the product team was present, not just monitoring, but engaging, they responded. Within a week, that member's insight had turned into a new prototype. Two weeks later, it was live.

That's not just product iteration. That's **co-creation**. And it's only possible in communities where trust moves faster than bureaucracy.

What makes this kind of development powerful isn't just the speed. It's the **fidelity**. When you're working inside a community, the signal is richer. It's not a binary of "like" or "don't like." It's layered. You see what people try. You hear what they compare it to. You get the emotional subtext behind their choices. This depth of insight is what makes great products, not just functional, but **felt**.

The best community-led product teams know this. They don't wait for roadmap validation. They bake listening into the build. They invite contributors into their process, not as tokens, but as partners. Sometimes that means inviting a power user to stress test a new tool. Sometimes it means co-writing documentation with a community member who's already built five internal how-tos for their team. Sometimes it means simply being available, visible, reachable, and responsive in a Slack thread at the right time.

And it scales surprisingly well, not because every voice is acted on, but because the **signal quality gets better with every new relationship**. You don't need a thousand voices to shape the right feature. You need *ten individuals you can trust who genuinely care and are honest*.

In the next section, we'll explore the mechanics of this process. Not just the inspiration, but the actual structures, how to run early betas with community input, how to gather and synthesize feedback without losing the thread, and how to make decisions transparently when not every voice agrees.

Because product isn't just what you ship, it's what you choose to build together.

From Listening to Looping: Making Feedback Actionable

There's a big difference between being open to feedback and being built to receive it. Most companies fall into the first category. They nod when users speak. They collect survey data. They check the right boxes. But when you pull back the curtain, there's no clear place for that insight to go. It floats. It accumulates. It rarely lands where decisions are made.

Community-led product development requires a different kind of architecture. Not just cultural openness, but **operational intent**. A system that knows how to catch signals, trace them to value, and loop them back into action, without losing their original meaning in translation.

The loop begins **before the build**.

Most teams define a roadmap in isolation. Strategy sessions. Backlog grooming. Executive prioritization. At best, they'll validate with a handful of user interviews. But in a community-integrated model, the earliest inputs come from the edge, not the center. The ideas that surface at the fringe of use cases come from various sources: power users pushing limits, new members struggling with onboarding, and contributors remixing the product in ways the original team never imagined.

These are not just anecdotes. They're **early signals of unmet need**. And when captured early, through discussion threads, user groups, live jams, even casual DMs, they shape the build from day zero.

But collecting feedback is only the beginning. What matters more is **how it's held.**

Strong teams create lightweight rituals for synthesis. Weekly community summaries. Dedicated "signal interpreters." Tags that differentiate a bug from a wish from an actual pain point. Internal discussions that don't just evaluate suggestions but **explain why decisions were made.** That kind of transparency builds trust. And trust turns passive members into active contributors.

This is especially powerful **during the build phase.**

It's easy to think of product creation as a time to close the gates. But for community-led companies, this is the moment to open them, carefully, deliberately. Running closed betas with known contributors. Sharing early prototypes in trusted spaces. Not to outsource QA, but to **co-locate perspective.**

When someone who helped shape the idea gets to see it live, even rough, they don't just give feedback. They advocate. They improve the work. They notice things a PM might miss, not because they're smarter, but because they live **closer to the edge of use.**

And they do so with generosity, not as critics, but as **co-authors of a shared toolset.**

Even after the launch, the loop continues. Community insight doesn't stop when the release hits production. In many ways, it intensifies because this is when real behavior emerges. Who's using it? How? What patterns repeat? What unexpected barriers surface? What new questions are being asked in public that weren't visible in testing?

The mistake many teams make is to move on too quickly. They declare the feature shipped. They check the box. But in a community-driven model, the release is not the finish line. It's the **start of the next round of learning**.

And when members see that their input shaped not just what was built, but how it evolves, something shifts. The product stops feeling like a service and starts feeling like **a space they help shape**.

That's when loyalty deepens, not because of retention campaigns, but because of **creative intimacy**.

In the next section, we'll explore real examples of this process in motion, how leading teams build co-creation pathways, avoid decision gridlock, and create rituals of participation that scale with the community's growth.

Because when feedback becomes partnership, and partnership becomes practice, the community stops being an asset. It becomes your **product advantage**.

Rituals of Co-Creation: How Community Shapes the Build

One of the clearest signals that a company is serious about community-led development is whether they've built rituals, not just ad hoc feedback moments, but *intentional practices* that signal: we're listening, we're building with you, and this process belongs to all of us.

At Figma, for instance, product managers didn't just lurk in their forums; they actively joined conversations, sometimes jumping into early plugin threads and responding like participants, not gatekeepers. They ran "community showcases" where contributors could share prototypes and friction points before features were even scoped. And when something made it from community request to public roadmap to release, it was acknowledged openly, not just in a changelog, but through celebration.

That celebration matters. It turns product improvement into **collective pride**.

Notion, similarly, leaned into community as a signal amplifier. Early power users built templates, hacks, and integrations long before Notion itself prioritized them. Instead of absorbing those ideas into the core team and closing the loop, they amplified the contributors, highlighting their work, building pathways for collaboration, sometimes even hiring directly from that contributor base. Community wasn't just a pool of ideas. It became a **recruiting lane, a beta lab, a content engine**, and most of all, a product intuition layer.

But you don't have to be a household name to do this well. Smaller SaaS teams often do it with even more intimacy.

I worked with one early-stage dev platform that hosted monthly "Build Together" calls. These weren't polished webinars. They were messy, live working sessions. The PM or tech lead would share a Figma file or live code walkthrough, and community members would weigh in, asking real-time questions, poking holes in logic, and suggesting interface tweaks. At first, it felt risky. Would people show up? Would it spiral? But over time, it became a trusted ritual. And it made the product *feel lived in*, not just designed behind glass.

That's the thing with these rituals. They don't just improve the product. They **increase the surface area of belonging**.

A member who attends a roadmap session, even just once, feels closer to the work. A contributor whose idea is named in the release notes feels seen in a way no swag bag could match. A developer who sees a community-created script become an official template feels not just appreciated but *included in the arc of the company.*

These rituals create leverage. Because they don't rely on scale, they rely on **intimacy, visibility, and rhythm**.

And they're replicable.

You can run a monthly changelog livestream, highlighting both shipped features and the community voices that influenced them. You can maintain a "community-pulled" board in your internal tools, tagging insights with links to the original post or user. You can set up a trusted tester group, not a static list, but a rotating circle, so more people get the chance to shape what comes next.

What matters most is not the format. It's the **follow-through**.

When people see that showing up leads to impact, they show up more often. When they see that their ideas don't disappear into silence, they start offering them before they're even asked. When they see that someone like them, not an insider or influencer, can help shape something real, the wall between "company" and "community" dissolves a little more.

And what emerges is a new kind of collaboration. Not transactional. Not reactive. But **relational, rhythmic, and authentic**.

In the final section of this chapter, we'll talk about boundaries, because not every idea can ship, and not every contributor will agree. The hard part isn't inviting feedback. It's decided in public, without breaking trust.

Because true co-creation isn't about saying yes to everything, it's about saying no **with clarity and care**.

Saying No Without Losing the Room

The hardest part of community-led product work isn't ideation. It's **discernment**.

When a user shares an idea, especially one rooted in personal friction or long-time use, they're not just offering a feature request. They're exposing a little piece of their worldview. They're saying, "This matters to me. I trust you enough to say so." And if that idea is dismissed, or worse, ignored, it doesn't just land as a product decision. It lands as a personal slight.

Which is why how you **say no** may be the most essential part of the process.

In traditional product models, decisions are made behind the scenes. Trade-offs are documented in internal docs, priorities are ranked, and when something doesn't ship, no one outside the team knows what was even considered.

But in a community-integrated approach, that invisibility isn't possible, or desirable. The conversation happens in public. The ideas live in various places, such as threads, comments, jam boards, and forum posts. You can't pretend they didn't arrive. You can only choose how to respond.

And the response matters deeply.

A community that never hears "no" is not being taken seriously. It's being appeased.

A community that only hears "yes" is not being trusted. It's being managed.

Genuine respect comes not from agreement, but from **transparent stewardship**. From being willing to say: We heard you. Here's how we thought about it. Here's what we're prioritizing instead. And here's why.

That kind of explanation isn't a weakness. It's **relational clarity**. It shows that leadership isn't arbitrary. Those decisions aren't just top-down but thought-through. It also sets the tone for the community itself. When people see the team modeling thoughtful disagreement, it permits them to do the same with each other.

The best product communities don't expect consensus. They cultivate **alignment through understanding**. Not everyone has to agree. But they do need to know that their voice had a place in the room, even if the outcome didn't match their preference.

And when possible, they're shown other paths to impact.

An idea that doesn't ship as a core feature might still become a community-built extension, a hack, a workaround, or a learning resource. A rejected concept might evolve in public and come back stronger. And the person who offered it, if treated with care, often becomes **more engaged**, not less, because they've experienced the difference between being heard and being handled.

Of course, this only works if your internal teams are on board.

A community-led product approach doesn't mean turning your roadmap into a democracy. But it does mean building **the muscles to explain trade-offs publicly**, to co-author improvement with users, and to move with more shared context than most teams are used to. It requires emotional intelligence, narrative skill, and a willingness to sit in the tension that the community always brings.

Because communities don't just offer insight, they **hold you accountable** to your promises. They remember what you said you cared about. They reflect it.

And if you let them, they'll make your product better, not just in features, but in *ethos*.

In the next chapter, we'll turn our attention from product to growth, from the inner loop of co-creation to the outer loop of **advocacy, attraction, and scale.**

Because when the community is truly aligned with the product, something powerful happens:

Your users don't just adopt. They **evangelize.**

Chapter 12: Community-Led Growth

From Audience to Flywheel

Most growth strategies are built on extraction. The logic is simple: find a market, capture attention, convert users, and scale through paid channels. It works, until it doesn't. Costs rise, trust erodes, attention fractures. And what once scaled cleanly starts to stall.

Community-led growth plays by different rules. It doesn't begin with targeting. It starts with **belonging**.

When someone joins a community, not just as a passive observer, but as a participant, they're stepping into a space where value flows in multiple directions. They're not being sold to. They're being **seen, heard, and given space to contribute**. That shift, from audience to member, is what makes community-led growth so potent. Because when people feel like they belong, they don't just stay. They **invite others in**.

Growth becomes a **side effect of resonance**, not just reach.

You see it when a forum thread turns into a LinkedIn post that sparks ten new sign-ups, when a member hosts their event because the format inspired them. When an internal Slack mention leads to an entire team adopting your tool, not because of a demo, but because a peer shared how it helped them, none of this is orchestrated. But none of it is accidental, either.

It happens because the conditions are there. A clear purpose. A trusted culture. A value exchange that goes deeper than incentives. When those things align, you don't need to *manufacture* virality. You need to **make participation visible**.

That visibility is key.

Community-led growth doesn't happen in shadows. It happens in various public artifacts, including blog posts, event recaps, toolkits, screenshots, comments, and case studies. Not polished marketing copy, but the messy, human markers of real people doing meaningful things. When you spotlight those moments, not just the metrics, but the stories, you give others a reason to lean in.

That's where the **flywheel** begins.

A new member joins. They find value. They engage. Their story is shared. Others see it. They join. They engage. Their story is shared. And so it continues, not as a top-down campaign, but as a *self-reinforcing loop* powered by trust.

Of course, none of this happens by accident. While the energy is organic, the structure must be intentional. It's not enough to hope people talk. You have to create the **conditions that make talking feel natural, valuable, and worth someone's time**.

In the next section, we'll look at what those conditions are, how companies build ambassador programs, create content ecosystems, and enable members to grow the brand alongside them, not just underneath it.

Because community-led growth isn't about turning members into marketers, it's about amplifying belonging until it scales on its own.

Designing for Amplification

Organic growth doesn't mean accidental growth. It means **natural motion that's been carefully enabled**. Behind every fast-growing, community-powered brand is a deliberate structure, one that invites members not just to participate, but to **contribute visibly and expand the surface area of the story**.

One of the most effective patterns is the *ambassador model*. Not in the old-school sense of promotional influencers reciting talking points. But in the newer, more relational sense, trusted community members serve as local translators of your mission. Not just extending reach, but adapting, localizing, and making it real for new people in new places.

Good ambassador programs don't begin with perks. They start with **trust and alignment**. Who already speaks with authority in your ecosystem? Who's already mentoring newcomers, hosting meetups, and creating tutorials, all without being asked? Those people don't need a campaign. They need **infrastructure**.

And that infrastructure doesn't have to be complicated. It starts with recognition. A clear invitation. A name for the role. Access to inside conversations. Early looks at the roadmap. Maybe a Slack channel, a monthly sync, a badge, not as currency, but as clarity. Something that says: "You are seen. You are part of how we grow."

Once that structure exists, the growth unlock is massive.

Ambassadors write blog posts in their voice. They start language-specific groups. They host onboarding calls for their region. They show up in places your team can't. And they do it not because they were assigned, but because **they believe**.

The same principle applies to content. One of the most misunderstood levers in community-led growth is **member-created content**. Not user-generated in the passive sense. Created. Authored. Initiated by people who see something, try something, build something, and want to tell that story.

But most companies treat content as something to manage. Approve. Edit into compliance. Which, more often than not, flattens the very texture that made it valuable.

The teams that get this right treat content like **conversation artifacts**. They highlight interesting forum replies. Turn threads into public-facing explainers. Run "week in review" recaps sourced entirely from member activity. They don't just tell the community's story; they **mean it with the community**.

The result? A steady stream of authentic, resonant material that doesn't feel manufactured. It feels alive. And it draws others in, not through ads, but through **affinity**.

And when people see themselves reflected in the narrative, they're more likely to step forward. To write. To speak. To share. That's the loop. Participation becomes amplification. Amplification becomes momentum.

And momentum, when designed well, becomes **growth without force**.

In the next section, we'll explore how to track and sustain this kind of momentum. Not through dashboards of vanity metrics, but through signals of **activation, advocacy, and alignment**.

Because real growth doesn't just scale users, it scales **believers**.

Measuring Motion, Not Just Reach

The temptation in any growth conversation is to flatten the story to numbers. Pageviews. Shares. Referrals. These metrics can tell you how many people saw something, clicked something, or took action, but not why they did it or what they felt when they did. And in community-led growth, that's why everything.

Because the power of community isn't just about scale, it's **signal quality**.

So how do you measure motion without stripping it of meaning?

Start by tracking **activation, not just acquisition**. In a community context, a new signup means little on its own. What matters is how quickly someone moves from observer to participant. Did they ask a question? Attend an event? Reply to a post? Tag someone else? Those actions mark the beginning of relational motion. They show intent. They show **belonging beginning to take root**.

Then look at **advocacy behaviors**. Who's sharing ideas in public, not just in your space but in theirs? Who's linking to your tools from blog posts, mentioning your product in webinars, referencing your frameworks in conversations that happen far beyond your official channels?

That's the signal that your community isn't just a container. It's a **transmitter**. And what it's transmitting isn't just utility, it's **identity**. People share what they believe in. When someone shares your product *through the lens of their own story*, you're not just getting exposure. You're getting emotional. Carry.

But the deepest signal is **reciprocity**. It's not about how often someone shows up. It's about what they give, and what that giving invites in return. A member who writes one brilliant guide that sparks five spin-off posts, a community builder whose event creates new rituals for others to host; these are acts that multiply. Their influence is **networked, not just visible**.

These kinds of metrics aren't always clean. They don't fit neatly into quarterly dashboards. But they are **strategic assets**.

Because they show that your community isn't a funnel, it's a **flywheel**.

And flywheels don't just grow. They sustain.

The mistake many companies make is to over-engineer this. They create referral programs too early. They slap gamification onto spaces that were thriving without it. They force a layer of strategy on top of something that was already working at the pace of trust.

What works better, always, is to **amplify what's already happening**.

If people are hosting events, give them support. If they're writing, provide them with a spotlight. If they're referring others, don't just track it, thank them in public, show how it helped, and make it visible. The goal isn't to manufacture advocacy. It's about recognizing and reciprocating it.

Because in the end, people grow communities the same way they develop relationships: through mutual care, repeated moments of recognition, and **the slow accrual of trust**.

In the final section of this chapter, we'll explore how this kind of growth can stay healthy, how to protect the integrity of the culture while welcoming new waves of people, energy, and scale.

Because the most challenging part of community-led growth isn't getting it to start, it's making sure it doesn't break what made it work in the first place.

Scaling Without Fracture

The irony of community-led growth is that its success can become its greatest threat. As more people arrive, drawn by the signal of something special, the very texture of that thing begins to shift. What was intimate becomes noisy. What was shared language starts to fragment. Culture gets stretched thin. And if left unchecked, the trust that built the community begins to erode quietly.

This isn't inevitable. But it is natural.

And the communities that grow with integrity are the ones that **expect this tension** and build systems to meet it.

The first system is orientation. Not onboarding in the shallow, transactional sense. Orientation in the more profound sense, *helping new people understand not just what to do, but how to be here.* What matters? What norms guide interaction? What stories do long-timers tell each other? What does good participation look like, not just in output, but in posture?

Strong communities don't scale culture by accident. They **ritualize transmission**. They create welcome guides with context, not just instructions. They pair newcomers with seasoned members. They make origin stories part of the landscape, not nostalgia, but grounding.

This creates coherence. And coherence is what allows a community to expand without splintering.

The second system is **distributed stewardship**. As growth accelerates, it's tempting to centralize control. To tighten the reins. To create rules in response to edge cases. But community doesn't scale through control. It scales through **trust in the right people**.

That's why ambassador programs, working groups, and role cycles matter. They widen the circle of care. They ensure that leadership is not bottlenecked in a single team, but **spread across a network of capable, aligned stewards** who understand the nuances of the space and can carry the culture forward.

This doesn't just protect quality. It **amplifies resilience**. When conflict arises or energy dips, it's not just the core team reacting. It's a distributed immune system responding. And because that response is relational, not bureaucratic, it keeps people close.

Finally, a healthy scale means making peace with change. A community that grows will constantly evolve. Some norms will loosen. Some rituals will fade. Some voices will get louder, while others will get quieter. Trying to preserve the past at all costs often creates more fractures than flow.

The better move is to hold on to values, not just formats.

If your value is generosity, it can be demonstrated through a live Q&A or a curated resource document. If your value is curiosity, it might live in a feedback loop or a story circle. The form can shift. The spirit remains.

And when you articulate those values, out loud, in writing, in your decisions, new members absorb them not by mimicry, but by resonance. They see what matters, and they find their place inside it.

That's how scale works best in a community. Not by tightening the walls. But by **strengthening the foundation**, so that what's beautiful can expand without becoming brittle.

In the next chapter, we move from growth to **support and success**, from the question of how community scales visibility, to how it scales **care, learning, and trust** at the level of daily experience.

Because when people help each other, not just because they're told to, but because it feels natural, you don't just reduce support tickets. You build a culture of mutual success.

Chapter 13: Community-Led Support & Success

When Help Comes From Within

Every company, at some point, hits the support ceiling. The volume rises, the team can't keep up, and the inbox becomes a battlefield. The instinct is to hire, to automate, to build macros. And those things work, to a point. But they're not a solution. They're a **stopgap**.

The real solution comes from a different source: the community itself.

When community is fully integrated into your customer experience, support doesn't begin when someone submits a ticket. It starts the moment they realize **they're not alone**. That someone else has faced this issue, solved it, explained it, or is at least willing to walk with them through it.

That shift, from company-to-customer to **peer-to-peer care**, changes everything.

It makes support faster. Not because you've added agents, but because you've added **trustworthy pathways**. It makes answers more accessible. Not because you've updated your docs, but because someone turned a workaround into a tutorial, and a tutorial into a conversation. It even makes failure feel lighter. Because when a user hits a wall and finds a real person, not a form, their frustration turns into **shared curiosity**.

This kind of community-led support doesn't emerge by accident. It requires **intention, design, and cultural clarity**. You're not just asking people to answer questions. You're building a system where helping others feels natural, rewarding, and even joyful.

At the heart of that system is **reciprocity**.

Most traditional support is transactional: you ask, we answer. But in a healthy community, support is cyclical. You get help, and eventually, you give it. Maybe not today. Maybe not on the same issue. But the loop stays open. And over time, that loop becomes **a living knowledge base**, shaped by real-world use and real-time need.

The difference in tone is palpable. In a help center, you read. In a community, you **listen**. You hear the voices. You feel the tone. You see the offhand jokes, the gentle nudges, the moments of empathy when someone says, "Yeah, that happened to me too. Here's how I fixed it."

That kind of support creates more than satisfaction. It creates **confidence**.

Not just in the product, but in the people around it.

And that confidence, in turn, becomes its success metric. Not just "Was your issue resolved?" but "Do you feel supported? Empowered? Part of something smarter than just one team behind one login screen?"

That's the deeper promise of community-led success: a model where knowledge, encouragement, and guidance don't bottleneck at HQ; they **circulate among peers**, constantly refreshed, constantly evolving.

In the next section, we'll explore the mechanics of that system and how companies design communities to enable real support at scale. What roles emerge? What patterns sustain the flow? And what it takes to turn your community into a **trusted infrastructure of help and success**.

Because support isn't a department, it's a **relationship model**. And when the community holds it, that relationship becomes **a shared victory**.

Building the System Around the Help

If you watch a thriving support community long enough, a pattern emerges. There's a pulse, a rhythm. Someone asks a question. Someone else answers. Another chimes in to clarify: a fourth links a resource, sometimes one they made themselves. The thread closes with thanks, or a reaction, or a quiet signal that things now make sense.

No ticket. No escalation. No backlog.

What you're seeing is a **self-sustaining loop of generosity**, and behind that loop, a system designed to keep it alive.

It usually starts with tone. Not policies, not permissions, **tone**. The first few people who answer questions set the culture. Are they kind? Clear? Curious? Do they shut down ambiguity or welcome it? Are they quoting documentation, or speaking from lived experience?

The tone you tolerate becomes the tone you scale.

That's why many successful communities seed early answers intentionally. Core team members or trusted contributors step in, not to dominate the conversation, but to **model it**. They show how to answer with care. How to link without condescension. How to turn a "wrong" question into a more profound moment of teaching.

That modeling creates safety. And safety is what invites more people to step in. Because most folks don't avoid answering questions out of laziness, they avoid them out of fear. Fear of getting it wrong, of being judged, of looking foolish. A warm, welcoming baseline removes that fear. And the more people answer, the more the **burden spreads**.

That's the second layer: **role clarity**.

Over time, in healthy communities, informal roles emerge. Some people become fast responders. Others become the deep explainers. Some specialize in edge cases. Others are helping total newcomers. These aren't assigned roles. They're earned ones, through repetition, reliability, and resonance.

Strong communities find ways to acknowledge those roles. Not with rigid titles, but with **social signals**. A shoutout in a community update. A "member spotlight." A little visual nudge, emoji, label, thank-you, that signals: your effort matters here.

These signals create reinforcement, not in the gamified sense of competition, but in the *human sense of recognition*. People keep helping because they see that it helps. And because they know they're not alone in doing it.

Underneath it all, you'll often find **community managers acting as connective tissue**, not answering every question, but noticing who is surfacing unanswered threads. Nudging the right person to weigh in. DMs, nudges, tags. Quiet but critical work. It's not glamorous. But it's how the system stays fluid.

And then there's the architecture: where this all happens. The best support spaces are **designed for motion**. Clear categories. Pinned guides. Templates for asking better questions. Spaces where experts and newcomers can coexist without noise. It's not about perfect design. It's about **removing friction** so help can move.

You can't force participation. But you can remove what blocks it.

In the next section, we'll explore how community-led support doesn't just solve problems, it **prevents them, and how** it becomes a surface for early detection, pattern recognition, and product insight.

Because when your users are helping each other, they're not just reducing your workload. They're building collective intelligence.

The Support Surface Becomes a Sensor

It starts with a question. "Has anyone else run into this?" Sometimes it's a bug. Sometimes a behavior. Sometimes just a feeling, something not quite working, something more complicated than it should be. In traditional support, that moment stays invisible until it turns into a trend. By then, you're already behind.

But in a thriving community, that question is **a signal**, early, raw, and rich with possibility.

That's the hidden value of community-led support: it doesn't just resolve issues. It **reveals them sooner before** they clog the inbox. Before they damage trust. Before they metastasize into churn.

And the best teams know how to listen.

They don't just track how many questions get answered. They pay attention to *which* questions keep reappearing. What metaphors are users using? What they're misunderstanding. What they're building workarounds for. Every one of those signals is a hint, not just at what's broken, but at what the product is *really like to use.*

A support ticket tells you something is wrong. A community thread tells you **why it feels that way**.

Over time, those threads become a kind of living map, a user-centric narrative of where your product needs to go. And if you're paying attention, you can act before the pain compounds.

Some teams systematize this. Weekly "insight harvests" from moderators or community managers. Tags and threads categorized by friction themes. Direct pipelines from community to product, where real member language, not sanitized summaries, gets reviewed at roadmap planning sessions.

Others use rituals, like "Pattern Fridays," where teams read the week's top posts out loud. Or "Slack Mirrors," where key community moments are surfaced directly into internal channels for designers and engineers to see. These aren't dashboards. They're **mirrors of reality**, designed to collapse the distance between builders and users.

What emerges is something rare: **anticipatory support**.

Before a feature confuses, someone's already made a guide. Before a change disrupts, a member has explained it in simpler terms. Before the flood of questions arrives, an event is hosted, a walkthrough is shared, and a shared language is formed.

This kind of proactive care isn't just helpful, it's *magnetic*. People stick around when they feel seen. When the space around them seems to anticipate their needs, and they realize that being part of the community means more than just getting help —it means **being part of the collective intelligence that improves the whole**.

And from the company's side, the benefit compounds. Every avoided support ticket. Every reduced onboarding bottleneck. Every insight that gets turned into clarity. These aren't just savings. They offer strategic advantages, enabling the business to move faster, with less friction, and more trust.

In the final section of this chapter, we'll explore how to maintain this dynamic as the community scales, how to avoid burnout, preserve quality, and protect the emotional bandwidth of those who show up to help.

Because support, when it's human, takes energy. And the more value it creates, the more **care it requires in return**.

Sustaining the System That Sustains You

The people who step up first, the ones who reply, clarify, and reassure, aren't doing it for points. They're doing it because they care. About the product, the people, the experience. They see something worth protecting, and they choose to help protect it. Again and again.

But even the most generous engines run low.

Over time, without structure, even vibrant support communities can fray. Contributors burn out. Experts grow tired of repeating themselves. Newer members struggle to step in. The culture gets brittle. The signal starts to fade.

Sustainable support doesn't just mean solving user problems. It means **supporting the people who help others**.

That begins with recognition. Not just in public thank-yous or leaderboard callouts, but in *quiet, consistent gratitude*. A DM that says, "I saw what you did there." A note from a product manager after a tough thread. A comment that links to a past post and says, "Still the best answer we've got."

This kind of recognition isn't performative. It's **relational reinforcement**. It tells someone: you're not just useful. You're valued.

Beyond recognition, the system itself must be designed for sustainability. That means rotating roles. Creating documentation to prevent experts from duplicating efforts and establishing mentorship structures that allow newer members to learn how to assist, gradually, safely, and at the right pace.

It means permission to pause. A culture where stepping back is not seen as failure, but as **part of the cycle**. The communities that last longest are the ones where care isn't just extended outward, but inward, too.

And it means offering real resources. That might look like stipends for moderators, early access to tools, or shared ownership in decisions that shape the space. It might mean a direct line to the support or product team, so high contributors don't feel like they're doing unpaid labor in a vacuum.

None of this turns support into a job. It simply **makes it sustainable**. So that people can keep showing up with their whole selves, without burning out or fading away.

And when they do step back, because life happens, and rhythms change, the structure holds. New people rise. Knowledge persists. Culture stays intact because you didn't build a dependency.

You built **a fabric**.

One held together by care, by clarity, and by trust.

In the next chapter, we'll explore how that same fabric can extend beyond support, into hiring, onboarding, and culture itself. Where your community doesn't just help you serve customers...

...it helps you grow your team.

Chapter 14: Community-Led Hiring & Culture

When the Community Becomes the Team

It happens quietly, at first. A power user offers feedback so sharp it feels like product strategy. A contributor shows up in forums with more consistency than some full-timers. A local chapter lead organizes events with more precision than the company's ops. You start to notice a pattern: the people who are building *with* you aren't on payroll, but maybe they should be.

That's the moment when a community shifts from being outside the company to becoming part of its **inner life**.

And if you're paying attention, that moment can change how you grow forever.

Community-led hiring isn't just about talent discovery. It's about **values alignment at scale**. When someone's been active in your ecosystem, building, helping, contributing, they haven't just demonstrated skill. They've shown **fit**. They understand your product. They've already earned the trust of others. They know the rhythm, the tone, the trade-offs.

Bringing them into the team doesn't require onboarding into the culture. It's a **continuation**, not a translation.

This is especially powerful in early-stage or fast-scaling teams, where every hire reshapes the company. Traditional hiring processes can catch credentials. They can test for competence. But they rarely reveal how someone *lives the work*. That's what community surfaces: not just what someone can do, but **what they're already doing, unprompted**.

And the relationship isn't just one-way.

When members see that their contributions can lead to opportunities, such as helping others, hosting events, or creating resources, they engage more deeply, not less. Not because they expect a job. But because they see a path. A real one. One where effort isn't extracted, it's **recognized, reciprocated, and, when right, invited in**.

I've seen companies hire support leads directly from their community forums. Designers from user showcase threads. Engineers who started by submitting API suggestions. These weren't employed as exceptions. They were hired as *evidence* that the community isn't just a marketing function. It's **a talent network in motion**.

In the next section, we'll look at how this dynamic plays out operationally, how to build hiring pipelines that include community, what signals to look for, and how to avoid the trap of tokenizing contributors.

Because community-led hiring only works when it's done with integrity.

When it's not about favors or shortcuts, but about recognizing who's already helping build the future you want to grow into.

Hiring With, Not From, the Community

There's a subtle but essential distinction between hiring from the community and hiring **with** the community.

Hiring *from* the community suggests extraction: scanning for top performers, plucking talent as if from a shelf. But hiring *with* the community means something more profound. It means treating the ecosystem not as a talent pool, but as **a lens**, one that helps you identify alignment, observe values in action, and invite new energy without disrupting the trust that makes the space work.

That process starts long before a job is posted.

In community-centered companies, hiring often begins with noticing. A contributor starts answering support questions with increasing clarity. A power user creates a tool that solves problems your team hasn't prioritized yet. A consistent voice in governance threads begins surfacing patterns others miss. These aren't job interviews; they're **visible demonstrations of judgment, care, and initiative**.

When those signals become steady enough, the conversation shifts. Someone inside the team says, "They're already doing the work. Should we talk?"

But this is where care matters. Because if that invitation is mishandled, if it's clumsy, extractive, or seen as a shortcut around a real process, you risk rupturing the very dynamic that made the person visible in the first place.

That's why the best community-hiring pipelines are **open but rigorous**.

They don't bypass the process. They integrate new inputs into it. A contributor might still go through a structured interview. They might still do a project or meet the wider team; what changes is not the *bar*, but the *context*. You've already seen how they show up. You're evaluating not just skill, but **compatibility with how things already move inside the system**.

And that evaluation goes both ways.

People in your community aren't auditioning. They're **participating**. If you reach out and offer a role, it should be with the understanding that they may not want it. That they may prefer to contribute with freedom. Not everyone needs to be pulled inside the walls to have an impact.

In some cases, the offer may not be a job, but a **shared responsibility**: a contract, a project, a stipend-backed ambassador role. Something that deepens connection without collapsing distinction.

This is especially important in diverse communities, where historical inequities may shape how authority is perceived and how opportunities are approached. If you want to truly hire with your community, you must make the path **transparent, invitational, and safe**. That means clear criteria. Respectful outreach. A process that includes, not overrides, the relationship.

You'll also need boundaries.

Just because someone contributes doesn't mean they're right for a full-time role. And just because someone applies doesn't mean they're ready for leadership. Saying no, in these moments, is as critical as saying yes. But it must be done **with care and context**, so the person remains a participant, not a disappointed applicant who vanishes.

This is the line community-led hiring walks: between invitation and intention. Between visibility and rigor. Between fast trust and long-term accountability.

When done well, it's powerful. It creates a culture where people know they can grow *into* the team, not through networking games or referral favors, but through **proximity, consistency, and aligned contribution**.

In the next section, we'll explore how these same principles shape **internal culture**, how community values outside the walls begin to rewrite what it means to work together inside them.

Because the ultimate promise of community-led hiring isn't better headcount, it's a more human way to build a company.

When the Inside Starts to Feel Like the Outside

There's a quiet moment that happens in many community-led companies, often unnoticed, but deeply felt. A new team member, just hired from within the community, joins their first internal call. They're surrounded now by the "inside." The team. The Slack. The calendar. But instead of trying to adapt to some alien culture, they feel something uncanny.

This already feels familiar.

The way people talk. The language. The references. The rhythms. Even the priorities.

It's not that they're insiders now. It's that the **inside reflects the outside**. The values they saw modeled in the community are real here, too. Not just branding, but behavior. Not just stated principles but *practiced ones*.

That alignment is rare. And when it happens, something powerful unlocks culture, becoming **porous in the best way**.

Instead of building walls between the company and the community, you're building **bridges**, ways for values, ideas, and rituals to travel back and forth, strengthening both sides.

This doesn't mean there's no distinction. A company still has to operate, to make hard calls, to hold private conversations. But when community values are deeply integrated, the internal culture shifts from performative to **participatory**. It becomes less about management, more about **stewardship**.

You see it in how decisions are made. Leaders reference community signals when discussing priorities. Designers include real user quotes in sprint planning. Engineers read forum threads before committing to architectural trade-offs. It's not pandering, it's proximity. It's **building with context, not just conviction**.

You see it in how people lead. Managers don't just manage tasks; they **narrate choices**. They communicate trade-offs transparently. They model vulnerability, knowing that leadership in a community-informed company isn't about perfection. It's about **credibility earned in motion**.

And you see it in how conflict is handled. Not by hiding behind HR templates or opaque decision trees. However, by returning to shared principles, mutual respect, clear accountability, and open dialogue, we can achieve a more effective outcome. The same practices that make a community strong are now **making the company resilient**.

One founder I worked with used to say, "If the people closest to our product don't recognize our internal culture, we've failed." What he meant wasn't that your community should run your company. It was that if your community wouldn't trust your internal behavior, you're building a house on shallow ground.

The companies that do this well treat internal culture not as an HR asset, but as **a reflection of the trust they're asking others to extend**.

When your internal rituals, standups, retrospectives, reviews, and external initiatives like community calls, AMAs, and roadmaps align, people stop feeling like they're moving between two worlds.

They start to feel like they're part of **one living, breathing ecosystem**.

In the final section of this chapter, we'll explore how that ecosystem becomes a long-term advantage, not just for hiring and culture, but for **resilience, retention, and the deep sense of belonging that builds companies people don't want to leave.** Because culture doesn't come from slogans, it comes from **shared memory, lived values, and open participation.**

Belonging as a Retention Strategy

The most significant risk in fast-growing companies isn't the hiring gap. It's the **drift**, that slow, almost imperceptible widening between who the company says it is, and how it feels to be inside. Teams get bigger. Processes calcify. Culture slogans get laminated and lose their meaning. New hires feel like passengers, not participants.

And over time, the center stops holding.

But in community-led companies, that drift is harder to ignore, because the **outside is always watching**, and the inside is always listening. You can't pretend to be people-first externally while allowing dysfunction to calcify inside. The membrane is too thin. Too alive. Too interconnected.

And that's a good thing.

It means the pressure to align is constant. It means the company must keep earning its narrative. And when done well, that pressure doesn't constrain. It **clarifies**. It sharpens the values that matter. It rewards behavior that reinforces trust. And it filters out those who are only here for short-term gain.

Because in a community-shaped company, culture isn't just a retention tool.

It's a shared container of meaning.

People stay in these environments not because they have to, or because the perks are good, or because the equity might pop.

They stay because the work feels **congruent**. Because the feedback loop between contribution and recognition is fast and human. Because they know what the company stands for, and they've seen it live, both inside and out.

This sense of coherence becomes magnetic. People talk about their jobs like they talk about their communities: with pride, with nuance, with story. They refer their friends, not because there's a bonus, but because they trust the environment. They write posts about their work not because they were asked to, but because it feels **worth narrating**.

And when they do leave, which they sometimes will, they stay close. They remain active in the community. They help the next generation. They cheer from the sidelines. Because their relationship to the company was never just economic, it was **relational**. It was cultural. It was **communal**.

That's the real legacy of community-led culture: it creates continuity.

People come and go, roles evolve, markets shift, but the core remains. A set of values. A network of trust. A rhythm of communication. And a **sense of shared authorship** in whatever happens next.

In the next chapter, we shift from culture to capital, examining how community-led businesses monetize and how they think differently about value creation, extraction, and sustainability.

Because when the community sits at the center of your business, you don't just make money *from* your users. You make money **with** them.

Chapter 15: Monetization

Not Just Revenue, Reciprocity

For most businesses, monetization is the engine room. It runs on spreadsheets and churn models, CAC and LTV, funnels and forecasts. These tools are helpful, even essential. But they were designed for a different kind of business, a business where value is extracted, optimized, and scaled like an industrial process.

Community-led businesses operate with a different logic.

Here, monetization is not just a function of conversion. It's a question of **reciprocity**. What are we giving? What are we earning? What are we sustaining, together?

That doesn't mean revenue doesn't matter. It means that **how** you earn matters just as much as what you earn. Because in a community, every transaction is also a **signal**. A piece of social context. A message about what kind of relationship you're inviting.

Charge too early, and you risk closing doors before value can circulate. Charge without clarity, and you confuse or alienate the very people who might have helped you grow. But when you get it right, when the way you monetize reflects your values, your trust, and your rhythm, the business becomes **stronger, not just bigger**.

There are two primary approaches to monetizing in community-led models: **direct and indirect**. The direct path is familiar: subscriptions, memberships, course fees, paid events, and product tiers. The user pays, the company delivers, the value flows cleanly. But even here, the community shifts the terms. The product isn't just software. It's access. Participation. Belonging.

A well-structured membership isn't a paywall; it's **an invitation to deeper collaboration**.

The indirect path is more subtle. The user doesn't pay directly, but their presence, participation, or advocacy creates value elsewhere. Perhaps they create content that attracts new users. Possibly, they offer support that reduces churn. Maybe their engagement surfaces product insights that accelerate roadmap velocity. In this model, **community becomes the growth engine, the retention lever, and the trust layer**.

And trust, once built, becomes a business multiplier.

Companies like Notion and Figma didn't monetize the community directly in the early stages. They capitalized on the momentum generated by the community. Every shared template. Every open-source plugin. Every YouTube tutorial. These weren't just signs of fandom. They were economic signals, evidence of a durable, scalable, self-reinforcing network.

But monetizing that kind of energy doesn't mean capturing it all. It means deciding **what to monetize and what to let circulate freely**.

In the next section, we'll explore how community-led businesses design pricing models that respect contribution, reward stewardship, and scale in rhythm with participation, not despite it.

Because in these ecosystems, money isn't just fuel. It's a reflection of mutual trust.

Designing Revenue in Rhythm with Participation

Pricing is never just a number. It's a story.

When someone pays for something, access, insight, tools, and community, they're not simply completing a transaction. They're signaling belief. Alignment. Trust. And in community-centric businesses, the way that pricing is framed, structured, and surfaced can either deepen that trust or quietly erode it.

Which is why the most successful community-led businesses don't just ask, "What can we charge for?" They ask, **"What are we asking people to believe in?"**

Some make this belief tangible through **tiered access**. A free level that welcomes all, open forums, starter tools, curated resources, and paid tiers that unlock deeper engagement. Not gated behind scarcity but structured like a ladder. Each tier reflects a new kind of participation: more access, more intimacy, more direct collaboration.

This isn't freemium in the traditional sense. It's **graduated belonging**.

The user isn't being nudged to upgrade with friction or popups. They're **growing into the next level** because their relationship to the ecosystem is deepening. Maybe they've found their people. Maybe they're running a local chapter. Perhaps they want to help shape the roadmap or host a workshop. The payment is a vote of confidence, not just in the product, but in the *community itself.*

Others use **pay-what-you-want models**, especially in creator-led or learning communities. These work best when there's already deep trust. When the audience isn't just an audience, but a group that feels **seen and respected, here**, the logic is simple: the value is real, and we trust you to contribute what you can.

You might lose some margin. But you gain something more complex to measure, **mutual regard**.

Still others offer **time-based access**, seasonal memberships, cohorts, and limited-run circles. These offer a rhythm, a beginning, middle, and end. People join not for a product, but for a **shared journey**. These models often pair well with learning or transformation-driven communities, where the product *is* the experience.

And then there's the hybrid path: indirect monetization. In these cases, the community isn't paying directly, but their actions drive revenue elsewhere. A Slack group that supports a SaaS product. A content library that drives SEO for a consulting business. A lively Discord community serves as the foundation for a hiring platform or cohort-based course.

The challenge in these models is **preserving clarity**.

When the community is not the product, you have to be crystal clear about the value exchange. Why are people here? What are you promising them? How do they benefit from the energy they contribute?

Because if people begin to feel like they are **the product**, rather than participants in a shared system, trust fractures. The moment someone realizes they're generating value for someone else without any recognition or reward, the flywheel stalls.

That's why sustainable monetization in community-led businesses depends not just on pricing, but on **perception**.

Not just what people pay. But how do they feel when they do?

In the next section, we'll explore how to balance direct and indirect monetization, reward contributors without over-engineering, and ensure that as money flows, **the spirit of the community remains intact**.

Because in these businesses, revenue is not just the goal. It's **the echo of alignment**.

Paying Without Poisoning the Well

Contribution is a fragile thing.

At first, it shows up freely: someone answers a question, writes a guide, hosts an event, builds a template. They do it because they care. Because they found something meaningful. Because it felt good to give. But the moment money enters the picture, everything changes.

Not always for the worse, but always in ways that must be handled with care.

In community-led ecosystems, the question isn't just whether to reward contributors. It's how to do it **without distorting the spirit of contribution itself**.

Not all value must be paid in currency. Recognition, access, influence- these are real forms of compensation, a contributor featured in the newsletter. A moderator is given a seat in product planning. A longtime member was invited to co-host a podcast episode. These gestures may cost little, but their impact can be profound. They affirm: *You matter. This is yours too.*

But there are moments when monetary value is appropriate, and even necessary, when a contributor's work replaces what would otherwise be done by the team. When someone creates ongoing infrastructure that others rely on, it can be a significant benefit when their labor becomes part of the product's perceived value.

In those cases, compensation is not just ethical. It's **strategic**.

Some communities use small grants or bounties: $250 for a new onboarding guide, $500 for hosting a local event. Others offer rev share, especially in marketplaces or tool-driven platforms. The logic is simple: if you create value, you share in what that value generates.

And then there are **formal contributor programs**: stipends, part-time roles, or structured fellowships. These programs work best when the expectations are clear, the time horizon is bounded, and the relationship is framed as a partnership, not piecemeal gig work, and not a backdoor to employment.

The key in all these models is **transparency**.

People need to understand what's rewarded, why it's rewarded, and how it's achieved. They need to trust that contributions are recognized **consistently**, not just based on proximity to leadership. They need to understand the terms, not just the money, but the meaning behind it.

Because if someone contributes expecting recognition or pay and gets silence instead, they don't just feel unpaid. They feel **unseen**. And that rupture is more complicated to repair than any missed transaction.

This is why monetization models in community-centric businesses require **a broader lens on value**. You're not just asking what's profitable. You're asking: What strengthens the fabric? What aligns with our values? What scales without corroding the very dynamic we depend on?

When the answers are honest, coherent, and public, people don't resent monetization.

They *respect* it.

Because they see themselves not as customers or users, but as **co-creators** of something worth sustaining.

In the final section of this chapter, we'll look at long-term sustainability: how to evolve monetization as the community matures, how to avoid over-commercialization, and how to preserve belonging even as the business grows.

Because in the end, the best community-led businesses don't just generate revenue. They **create value that outlives the transaction**.

Sustaining Value Without Sacrificing Trust

At some point, every community-led business reaches a fork in the road. Growth accelerates. Budgets tighten or expand. Investors ask different questions. And the impulse creeps in: **"How do we monetize this more aggressively?"**

It's a fair question. But if answered poorly, it becomes the first crack in a much deeper fracture.

Because the community wasn't built on extraction, it was built on **alignment**, on shared values, reciprocity, and the quiet rituals that made it feel like more than just a customer base.

So how do you grow revenue without breaking the thing that made revenue possible in the first place?

The first answer is **clarity of purpose**. A community that exists to help creators grow will tolerate the monetization of workshops or resources. A developer ecosystem may happily pay for advanced tools. But if the tone suddenly shifts, and what was once a free, exploratory space becomes riddled with upsells or gated behind tiers, people notice. And they leave.

Long-term monetization depends on honoring the original social contract.

That means preserving generous surface area, spaces where people can still learn, connect, and contribute freely. It means keeping a pulse on what the community *feels like*, not just what it earns. It means being honest about why something is paid, what it unlocks, and how that revenue supports the system as a whole.

Some teams write their philosophy out loud. "We charge for X so we can keep Y free." Others reinvest a percentage of revenue back into the community, funding events, supporting creators, and paying moderators. These moves aren't just ethical. They're **structural reinforcements**. They keep the ecosystem healthy by ensuring that revenue **flows through**, not just **up**.

The second answer is evolution with integrity.

As communities grow, their needs change. What once felt intimate becomes more complicated to manage. What was once simple becomes layered. This doesn't mean monetization must stay static. But it does mean changes should be made **in rhythm with the community's maturity**, not just the company's pressure.

Introducing a paid tier? Give plenty of lead time. Explain why. Show who benefits. Offer a path for longtime contributors. Adding sponsorships or partnerships? Vet them with the same care you expect members to bring to their contributions. Protect the tone. Protect the norms. Remember: your business may own the platform, but the community owns the **culture**.

And that culture is your greatest asset.

Because at its best, a community doesn't just tolerate your business model. It **believes in it**. People want to support what they helped build. They want it to last. They'll pay, not to unlock value, but to **keep value circulating**.

That's the difference between a customer base and a community. Customers transact. Communities **invest**.

And when you earn that investment, not just once, but repeatedly, in rhythm with what the community cares about, you don't just make money.

You make meaning. You create something that lasts.

In the next chapter, we move into the final phase of this book: the **playbooks, pitfalls, and future directions** that will shape how community-led strategy evolves from here. Because building community is not the goal, it's how we make what comes next.

Chapter 16: Community Strategy Playbooks

From Philosophy to Practice

Up to this point, we've explored the why and the what of community-led strategy, and why it matters now. What it looks like when it works. How it shapes growth, product, support, hiring, and even revenue. But for many teams, understanding the philosophy is only half the battle. The next question is always the same: **"How do we do this?"**

That's where the playbooks come in.

A playbook is not a checklist. It's not a plug-and-play system. In a community, there are too many variables — culture, context, timing, and tone — for anything to be truly universal. But what playbooks can do is offer **frames**. Repeatable patterns. A sense of where to start, what to expect, and how to adapt as you go.

The truth is, community-led strategy doesn't look the same for every business. A solo creator building a learning network has different needs than a SaaS platform with ten thousand active users. A two-sided marketplace has different dynamics from an open-source tool or a mission-driven nonprofit.

But each of these businesses can **center community** in how they grow. Each can find leverage not by scaling *to* their audience, but by scaling *with* their people.

The common thread is **intentional design**.

Community doesn't become strategic just by existing. It becomes strategic when it's mapped to real goals, resourced with care, and allowed to evolve in sync with the business. That means understanding where your community fits within your value chain, who it serves, how it operates, and what makes it vulnerable.

This chapter offers a set of applied lenses. Not templates, but trajectories. Scenarios for how different business types can build community into their core operations, from early formation to maturity.

Some of these playbooks will be familiar. Others might feel counterintuitive. But each one draws from real-world patterns, companies that have not just built community, but **grown through it**.

And if there's a single principle that binds them all, it's this: **start specific, scale from signal**.

Don't begin by trying to build a community for everyone. Begin by serving someone deeply. Solve for clarity, not size. Make one corner of your ecosystem thrive before expanding the map.

Because in community, as in strategy, **precision beats ambition every time**.

In the next section, we'll dive into the first archetype: the **early-stage SaaS company**, and how community can become its most significant advantage in product-market fit, retention, and early growth.

Playbook 1: Early-Stage SaaS – Build with, Not for

For most early-stage SaaS companies, the first strategic hill to climb is product-market fit. Does what we're building matter? Will people use it, tell others, stick around? Founders obsess over features, polish onboarding flows, and A/B test relentlessly. And still, many stalls, *not* because they lack a product, but because they're **building in isolation**.

That's where community becomes the hidden advantage, not as a channel to sell more, but as a surface for **faster learning**.

The earliest users in a SaaS environment are more than customers. They're co-developers, pattern detectors, and potential advocates. But only if you make space for them to behave that way.

The simplest way to begin is with **a shared space**. A Slack group, a forum, a Discord. Not for announcements, but for **real conversation**. This is where you start to see what people ask, what they struggle with, and what they expect that isn't there. These are the threads that no user interview can surface. Not abstractions. Friction, in real time.

But what makes this powerful isn't just the data, it's **the dynamic**.

When users help each other, they deepen their relationship with the product. When they see the team listening, responding, and adjusting, they go from being testers to *believers*. They start to use "we" when they talk about the roadmap. They share feedback not as complaints, but as **contributions to something they feel part of**.

That feeling, that shift from user to participant, is where the flywheel begins.

And from there, things compound. Someone shares a workaround that becomes a formal feature. Someone else writes a guide that gets embedded into onboarding. A third organizes a mini-event or live Q&A, not because they were asked, but because the product helped them solve something that mattered.

If you recognize these moments early and **amplify them with care**, they become the seeds of a culture. Not just "users who help," but **a community that grows alongside the product**.

The role of the team here is part builder, part host. You're shipping code, yes. But you're also narrating choices. Sharing drafts, asking fundamental questions in public, and accepting answers that might not always feel good. You're shaping a room where early adopters become **early authors** of the experience itself.

Some teams formalize this dynamic with contributor channels or feedback rituals, monthly roadmap reviews, feature voting, and changelog sessions. Others do it more quietly, with direct pings, private calls, or unstructured DMs that say, "What did you think?"

The format matters less than the **posture**. You're not asking for input to validate what you've already decided. You're building *with the community in the loop*. Not just because it's generous, but because it's **efficient**. It reduces blind spots. It derisks launches. It builds loyalty that marketing dollars can't buy.

In the next section, we'll explore how that same community, once formed, becomes your **engine for support and growth**, reducing costs, increasing retention, and driving referrals without relying on cold acquisition.

Because for SaaS founders, community isn't just a side channel. It's an accelerant for everything else.

From Users to Advocates: Community as Growth Loop

Once a community starts to take shape inside an early-stage SaaS company, the temptation is to treat it as a side benefit. A nice-to-have. Something to visit when marketing gets quiet or the product needs cheerleaders. But the most successful founders resist that framing. They know this is not *adjacent* to the business. It is the **engine behind everything else**.

The first signal of this shift is support.

You start to notice that new users are asking questions, but *you're not the one answering them anymore*. Another user steps in. Then another. Sometimes the responses are better than your docs, simpler, more transparent, more empathetic. A working thread begins to form: "Oh, I had that issue too, here's what I tried."

It's tempting to formalize that. Pin the best answers. Highlight top contributors. But the real move isn't control. It's **curation**. You don't try to govern the community like a ticketing queue. You try to **keep the water clear**, maintain low noise, provide high context, and adopt a tone that welcomes learning.

Support becomes less about scaling a team and more about **activating a network**. And as that network begins to trust itself, something else starts to happen: growth.

Someone writes a public review, not as an influencer, but as a real user with real use cases. Another person builds a Zapier integration and shares the template. A third posts a YouTube demo, complete with their commentary, quirks, and all. These moments aren't coordinated. They're **earned media**, but not in the PR sense.

They're proof of belief.

And when new users see those artifacts, not slick brand videos, but messy, real, human stories, they trust faster. They try sooner. They stay longer.

That's the loop.

Community helps users get started, stay supported, and become visible contributors. And visibility leads to influence, which leads to growth. Not a funnel. A **flywheel**, one that starts slow but compounds with every shared tutorial, solved problem, and answered question.

Retention, too, follows a different curve. People don't just stay because the product works. They stay because the product is **socially alive**. They know where to go when something breaks. They feel noticed when they give feedback. They see new ideas evolve in public, and feel, however subtly, like they're part of that motion.

And so, they give back. Not out of obligation, but out of *recognition*. A sense that this thing we're building matters. That it's not just software; it's a system with people in it. People like them—people they trust.

And in a market where churn is the default, that kind of attachment is not sentimental. It's **strategic armor**.

In the next section, we'll close the SaaS playbook with a look at *when to formalize roles, programs, and rituals*, and how to scale the culture without diluting what made it work in the first place.

Because community-led SaaS isn't just about launching a Slack group. It's about **stewarding a movement**.

Formalizing Without Freezing

At some point, the scale catches up with the story. What began as a scrappy group of early users has grown into something larger, with hundreds, maybe thousands of people. Threads move faster. Questions get repeated. The vibe starts to shift. It's not that things are worse. It's that they're **different**.

And the question becomes: How do we keep what made this work... *working*?

The instinct is to institutionalize. Build programs. Appoint moderators. Write guidelines. And yes, some of that is necessary. But if you do it too fast, or too rigidly, you risk freezing the very fluidity that gave the community life.

The better path is to formalize from a pattern, not pressure.

Watch what's already happening organically. Who's answering questions consistently? Who's starting helpful threads? Who's translating technical updates for newcomers in a human voice? Those people don't need titles. They need **support**— maybe a little access. Perhaps a direct line to the team would be helpful. Maybe just recognition.

Formalize what's already true.

One founder I spoke with framed it this way: "We don't create roles. We name them after they emerge." That meant giving people badges once they'd already shown leadership. It involved creating rituals, such as monthly contributor calls and changelog reviews, around behaviors that were already in motion.

Culture is scaled by reflecting, not projecting.

When it came time to build programs, the team was careful, involving ambassadors, experts, and even paid contributors. Not every contributor wanted structure. Some just wanted autonomy. Others wanted to level up into more responsibility. So the team created **multiple paths**, a spectrum of participation, some light, some deep, all transparent.

The key was optionality. And rhythm.

Roles came with clear time boundaries, seasonal cycles, opt-in periods, and renewal checkpoints. That way, no one burned out trying to "hold the vibe" forever. And the program stayed **alive to change**, not trapped in past dynamics.

As the company grew, the internal culture began to mirror the community's DNA. New hires were onboarded not just to tools, but to tone. Community health was tracked alongside revenue. Community contributors got seats at the roadmap table, not as a favor, but as a strategic input.

And most critically, the community wasn't seen as a department. It was understood as **an orientation**, a way of seeing the business not as a machine to be optimized, but as a network to be **tended**.

That orientation is what keeps the soul intact.

Because a product may be technically impressive, a growth curve may be steep. But what people remember, and what they stay for, is how a space made them feel, particularly if they felt useful or heard, if they felt **part of something that was building toward a shared good**.

For SaaS companies, that's the real unlock. Not just lower CAC or better NPS. But a company that grows because its community does.

In the next section, we'll shift to a new context: the **two-sided marketplace**. How community-led strategy functions when you're not serving one user group, but two, each with their own needs, incentives, and identities.

Because community doesn't just bind users, it **balances ecosystems.**

Playbook 2: Two-Sided Marketplaces

Every marketplace lives or dies by one dynamic: **trust between strangers**. Whether you're connecting hosts and guests, teachers and students, buyers and sellers, your platform isn't the value. The exchange is. And your job is to make that exchange safe, smooth, and worth returning to.

Community becomes critical not because it adds features, but because it **fills the gaps that code can't close**.

In a two-sided marketplace, those gaps are everywhere. The seller feels uncertain about whether their effort will pay off. The buyer wonders whether this is legit. The power users on one side are unsure how to contact the other. And when things go wrong, which they will, someone needs to explain, reassure, and recover.

This is where most marketplaces over-index on automation. Dispute resolution flows. Feedback loops. Escalation ladders. All useful. All necessary. But none of them builds trust. Not absolute, human trust.

That kind of trust is **cultural**, not transactional.

And community is how you shape that culture.

But unlike a single-audience company, marketplaces must navigate **two (or more) communities**, often with very different rhythms. The seller side might want education, pricing benchmarks, and tooling. The buyer side might wish for transparency, reviews, and a sense of belonging. If you treat the whole thing as one blob, you lose nuance. If you separate them, you lose cohesion.

The art is to design a shared identity without flattening individual needs.

One way to begin is by creating **mirrored community experiences** on each side: two forums, two event series, two onboarding paths, each tailored to the needs of that group. The seller side might have a tips-and-tools channel, mentorship circles, and quarterly showcases. The buyer side might have Q&A, product discovery threads, and curated user journeys.

But underneath those two paths, you begin weaving **everyday rituals**.

An annual event that brings both sides together. A shared narrative about what the platform enables. A set of shared values, honesty, creativity, and resilience, that transcend the roles people play. You're not just building two communities. You're building **a shared ecosystem with plural identities**.

And when that ecosystem works, magic happens.

Supply feels supported. Demand feels engaged. The platform doesn't feel like an intermediary; it feels like **a town square**. People return not just for utility, but because the space itself has meaning. A vibe. A story.

In the next section, we'll look at how marketplaces activate their early communities, build initial liquidity with humans at the center, and use **participation loops** to keep the system from stalling.

Because in a two-sided world, growth doesn't come from one group. It comes from the quality of the connection between both.

Seeding the Sides, Building the Bridge

Every marketplace begins lopsided.

Maybe you have a handful of sellers, but no buyers. Perhaps you've courted demand, but supply is weak. Maybe both sides exist, but they're mismatched, wrong categories, wrong geography, wrong expectations. And while algorithms and marketing can help, what the early-stage marketplace most desperately needs is **human energy**.

Community becomes the first thing that makes the space feel alive.

But it can't be treated like a broadcast. At this stage, your job is not to "build community" in the abstract. It's about matching-make with care, highlighting early wins, and sharing **what's working**.

Start with one side.

Often, it involves supply, creators, hosts, freelancers, and instructors. The people who do the work that others come for. Begin by **making them feel seen**. Invite them into a private space: a beta circle, a founding cohort, a community call. Not to sell them, to listen. Ask what they're building, what they need, what they're worried about.

Then do the work **manually**.

Help them create better listings. Review their first offers. Introduce them to others in the same space. This isn't scalable, and it's not supposed to be. You're creating *early momentum*, and more importantly, you're modeling the behavior you want this space to nurture.

That energy becomes contagious. The more people feel helped, the more they help others. And soon, you can step back and let the culture carry some of the load. That's when you bring in the other side, carefully.

Buyers, learners, seekers, they need a reason to show up. Not just because something is available, but because **something is happening**. Highlight real activity. Use community stories as marketing. "Here's what our top creators are offering this month." "Here's what our customers are loving." You're not pushing product. You're **narrating momentum**.

But perhaps most importantly, create *moments of overlap*. Webinars where sellers share insights with buyers. AMA sessions where buyers ask real questions. Features that highlight success stories on both ends. These touchpoints are where trust compounds. They demonstrate to both sides that this isn't just a transactional engine. It's **a space with intention**.

As both sides grow, lean into **reciprocal rituals**. A "seller of the month" profile is nice, but even better when it's paired with feedback from a delighted customer. A learning circle isn't just content; it's an activation tool for both demand *and* supply. The flywheel is fueled not just by what people do, but by **how visibly they do it for one another**.

You'll know the community is working when people stop asking, "What can I get?" and start asking, **"How can I contribute?"**

That's when your marketplace moves from fragile liquidity to a durable network.

In the next section, we'll explore how to **govern this dual-sided community at scale**, protecting tone, fairness, and momentum even as categories expand, incentives evolve, and edge cases multiply.

Because a thriving two-sided community doesn't just grow, it **balances itself in motion**.

Governing in Motion: Keeping the Culture Coherent

As a marketplace matures, the initial momentum that held it together begins to wane. New categories open up. New participants arrive with different expectations. Moderators who once knew everyone by name now oversee thousands of threads.

The original tone, the human warmth that sparked connection, risks being buried under scale.

This is where most communities falter. Not because they've lost interest, but because they've lost **coherence**.

The governance challenge in a two-sided marketplace is unique. You're not just protecting a single set of norms. You're navigating **dual identities**, often with different incentives, behaviors, and vocabularies. And you can't rely solely on platform rules or enforcement mechanisms to preserve trust.

The answer is culture, but not the kind you write down once and forget. This is a **living culture**, shaped as much by norms as by nudges, rituals, and visible reinforcement.

That starts with clarity. Not rules for rules' sake, but **shared expectations**. How do we treat one another here? What kinds of feedback are constructive? What happens when trust is broken? This clarity doesn't come from legal pages. It comes from modeling how early moderators respond, how the company shows up when something goes wrong, and how conflict is handled in the open.

In marketplaces, fairness is a sensitive axis. If sellers feel customers are coddled, they'll disengage. If buyers think the platform sides with sellers, they'll walk. The community must be stewarded as **a space of balanced accountability**. That doesn't mean neutrality; it means consistency.

Some platforms empower elected councils or "voice groups" from both sides to weigh in on policy changes. Others host regular town halls where feedback loops stay live. The method can vary. The principle is the same: **governance is not just control, it's participation**.

And as the platform grows, the best governance structures aren't imposed top-down. They are **grown from the behavior you want more of**.

Reward contributors who mediate disputes with grace. Highlight buyers who write thoughtful reviews. Celebrate sellers who support one another behind the scenes. When those stories become visible, they teach new members what's normal here. What's admirable. What gets remembered.

Of course, not every edge case can be solved by culture. Sometimes rules must be drawn. Harassment. Fraud. Abuse. But even then, enforcement should reflect values. Not reactive bans, but visible reasoning. Not performative discipline, but **community-protective clarity**.

Because people don't need perfection, they need to feel that the space **is actively cared for**.

That someone is watching. That someone will listen. That fairness is not arbitrary, but alive.

In the final part of this playbook, we'll explore how two-sided marketplaces turn long-term community engagement into **strategic defensibility**, a moat not made of code or capital, but of trust, belonging, and collective memory. Because what keeps users loyal isn't the lack of alternatives. It's the feeling that **this space is theirs**.

Community as Moat, Memory, and Meaning

In every crowded market, the pressure to differentiate intensifies. Competitors match features. Prices race downward. Margins erode. And the thing that once felt innovative starts to feel... replaceable.

But not all value is visible on the roadmap.

The most substantial marketplaces don't just survive by iterating faster. They endure because they've built something **competitors can't copy overnight**: a community that believes in itself.

That belief is the real moat.

It lives in the relationships formed between users, the rituals that give the platform identity, and the shared language that grows richer with each exchange. It's not locked in with contracts or exclusivity clauses. It's **held in memory, built through experience**.

You see it in the way people defend the platform, not because they were paid, but because they've been helped. You see it when power users advocate for improvements, not as critics, but as co-authors. You see it when newcomers are onboarded not by the company, but by members who remember what it felt like to be new.

These are not transactions. They are **traces of belonging**.

And when belonging is real, people don't leave just because a new feature launches elsewhere. They stay because this space understands them. They stay because they trust the tone, the process, the shared sense of fairness. They stay because their reputation, built over months or years, is entwined with the platform itself.

This is what the community offers: **inertia with meaning**. Not lock-in, but loyalty.

And that loyalty becomes leverage. In moments of change, policy shifts, price adjustments, and platform evolutions, it's the community that makes the difference between churn and adaptation. If people believe you're building with them, they'll adapt. If they don't, they'll resist or disappear.

Community is not a hedge against disruption. It is **the infrastructure of adaptability itself**.

And that's why the most enduring two-sided marketplaces invest in their community not as a marketing channel, but as **the living layer of trust** beneath everything else, because no competitor can replicate your early contributors. Your rituals. Your shared memories. Your invisible scaffolding of meaning.

Those things are slow to build and nearly impossible to fake.

In the next section, we'll explore the third applied playbook: **creator-led businesses**. These are solo or small-team companies where the founder *is* the brand, and community isn't just an asset, but a mirror, an amplifier, and often, **the product itself**. Because when the business is personal, the community is everything.

Playbook 3: Creator-Led Businesses

It begins with a voice. A point of view. A person says something true in public, and others respond, *"Yes, I feel that too."*

This is the seed of every creator-led business. Not a product, but a **presence**. A sense of connection. The creator shows up consistently, online, in newsletters, on podcasts, and over time, what began as an audience becomes something more. People don't just consume. They gather. They begin to **orbit**.

That's when the creator has a choice.

They can continue broadcasting, expanding their reach, refining their funnel, and selling products to a silent audience. Or they can build a community not just around them, but **with** them. An ecosystem where people don't just watch the creator, they find each other.

The shift is subtle but transformational. From: "I follow you. "To: "I've found my people here."

That's when a creator-led business becomes **community-powered**.

The early moves are light but intentional. A shared space, maybe a Discord, Circle, or private newsletter thread. A prompt that invites response. A cohort-based course where students meet each other, not just the teacher. A paid membership that isn't just access to content, but access to **each other**.

The creator's role begins to change. Less like a broadcaster. More like a host.

They still lead, but not every conversation. They still teach, but others begin to prepare, too. And slowly, something begins to shift: the community **gains its gravity**. New people arrive not just for the creator, but because they've heard *this is where the best conversations happen*. This is where others like them are doing the work, having the dialogue, living the values.

This is where content becomes context, where ideas become identity.

What makes this dynamic powerful isn't scale, it's intimacy. There is a sense that people are not performing here. They are exploring. And the creator, far from needing to carry it all, becomes a **facilitator of energy** that already exists.

In the next section, we'll explore how creators structure their communities for **depth over volume**, why small doesn't mean insignificant, and how sustainable models emerge from trust, participation, and meaningfully designed access.

In creator-led ecosystems, community isn't just about retention. Its **relevance**.

Designing for Depth, Not Just Reach

Most creators start by reaching out through a tweet, a podcast, or a blog post. And for a time, growth means more reach, more followers, more eyeballs, more traction. But eventually, the question changes. It becomes less about how many people see your work and more about who stays **and why**.

This is where community becomes not just a tactic, but a strategy.

Because if the audience is the crowd that listens, the community is the group that **builds the stage with you**. They show up not just to consume, but to contribute. They come back not just for you, but for each other. And what you're building together is not just content, it's **context**.

That kind of context doesn't scale like a newsletter. It grows **relationally**, through trust and rhythm, which is why creator-led communities thrive when they are **deliberately small**. Not exclusionary but **curated for coherence**.

That might mean a cohort of twenty in a private course. A membership cap of five hundred. A once-a-month call instead of a 24/7 forum. These boundaries don't limit your business. They **protect your intimacy**, which becomes the product itself.

You see this in thriving learning communities: one clear focus, tight facilitation, explicit norms, shared outcomes. You see it in creative networks, where members co-review work, exchange referrals, and share tools. You see it in identity-driven spaces, neurodivergent founders, climate-conscious designers, and indie app developers, where trust isn't a feature. It's **the infrastructure**.

Revenue, in these models, often flows from **participation, not passive access**.

People pay to be part of something where they are **seen and needed**. It might be a paid Slack, a course, a retreat, or a recurring mastermind. The container matters less than the **care with which it's held**. People aren't just buying knowledge. They're buying clarity, connection, and forward motion.

And the creator's job isn't to fill every silence or solve every problem. The goal is to create a **structure that others can move within**.

The most successful creator-led communities offer just enough form to feel held, and just enough freedom to feel empowered. A prompt. A rhythm. A tone that invites contribution without demanding performance.

And when someone shows up with energy, answers a question, shares a resource, comforts someone in doubt, the creator names it. Amplifies it. *"This is what this space is for."* Over time, that reinforcement becomes muscle memory. New members learn not from rules, but from **repetition of behavior they admire**.

In the next section, we'll explore how creator-led communities navigate **monetization**, balancing access, exclusivity, and generosity, while keeping the core community dynamic intact because the most resilient creator businesses don't just convert followers. They **cultivate stewards**.

Earning With, Not From

The hardest tension in any creator-led business is the same: how do you monetize without making people feel like they've become the product?

For most creators, the early days are powered by generosity. Free threads. Free videos. Long, thoughtful newsletters. And it works, because generosity builds trust. But generosity alone doesn't pay bills. And eventually, that tension rises: *How do I charge without breaking what made this valuable in the first place?*

In a traditional business, the answer is simple. You make something, and people pay for it. But in a community-centric creator business, the line isn't so clean. What you're offering isn't just knowledge or tools, it's access, belonging, participation. And people don't pay for those things the way they pay for a download.

They pay when the container feels alive.

That's why the most successful monetization strategies in creator communities feel **less like transactions and more like invitations**. You're not upselling, you're opening a door.

You might begin with free content, yes. But then offer a members-only call, where people can ask questions live, reflect together, or share their work. You might create a paid newsletter, but make it collaborative, with community highlights, reader questions, or guest segments from long-time members. You might run a workshop, not as a lecture, but as **a guided experience with shared outcomes**.

These offers don't compete with the free layer. They **deepen it**. They say: If you've found value here, come closer. Come into the room where the work gets richer.

And when the invitation is authentic, people don't feel sold to. They feel **seen**.

There's also space for higher-leverage plays. Annual memberships. Retreats. Inner circles. Small-group intensives. These are not mass-scale products. They're **experiences that scale meaning, not volume**. And that's why they work. Because people aren't just paying for information. They're investing in **transformation with others**.

But with every layer of monetization, one thing must stay clear: the line between **value and access**.

If people feel they can't belong unless they pay, you lose trust. If longtime contributors suddenly find themselves priced out of the space they helped build, you lose continuity. The best creators handle this with transparency: *Here's what's free. Here's what's paid. Here's why. And here's how each tier supports the whole.*

Sometimes this looks like scholarships. Sometimes it's pay-what-you-can. Sometimes it's letting longtime members in for free, because **their presence is part of the product**.

That kind of clarity is rare and powerful. It tells your community: you're not here to extract. You're here to **build something sustainable, together**.

In the final section of this playbook, we'll look at what happens when a creator business truly scales, and how to grow the ecosystem without diluting the tone, flattening the relationships, or over-engineering what was once deeply human. Because at scale, what you've built isn't just a community. It's **a living legacy**.

Scaling the Spirit

Growth is seductive. The metrics tick up: subscribers, members, revenue. People tell you it's time to "take things to the next level." Hire a team. Launch a platform. Build infrastructure. And yes, some of that might be necessary.

But in creator-led communities, scale is not neutral. It changes the texture of the room.

What was once small and spontaneous becomes scheduled. What was once a comment from the creator now passes through the staff. New members arrive faster than culture can catch them. And if you're not careful, something fragile begins to dissolve: **the sense that this space was built with me in mind**.

The challenge isn't avoiding growth. It's growing in rhythm with what made the community matter in the first place.

The best creator-founders scale **intentionally, not reactively**. They don't rush to industrialize intimacy. They **protect its**

structure. That might mean growing in seasons, open enrollment, rest periods, and rebalancing. It might mean layering the community, not expanding it: keeping a tight inner circle while creating lighter, broader edges for those just entering.

Think of it like a campfire.

There are people close to the flame, veterans, contributors, familiar voices. Their presence holds the heat. Beyond them, a second circle: engaged observers, new members watching the rhythm, deciding how close they want to get. And then the broader field, lurkers, followers, passersby who feel something meaningful is happening here, even if they haven't stepped in yet.

Your job isn't to pull everyone to the center. It's to **tend the fire**.

That means setting boundaries that are protective, not exclusionary. It means creating clear roles so new energy can be integrated without overwhelming what already works. It means letting others carry some of the cultural weight, by curating, hosting, and modeling tone, so it's not all on you.

Some creators step back from day-to-day community and focus on vision, curriculum, and storytelling. Others stay close to the center but **train stewards to hold the edges**. There's no one right way. But all sustainable paths share one quality: **they center coherence over control**.

They understand that a strong community doesn't need to be everywhere. It needs to feel like **a real place**.

And when that sense of place is preserved, when growth doesn't blur the boundaries but **reinforces the identity**, the business becomes more than the sum of its offerings.

It becomes a landmark. A place where people take pride in having found it early. A place people return to when everything else feels noisy or hollow.

And the creator? They become something rarer than viral. They become **trusted**.

In the next section, we'll begin the fourth playbook: for **mission-driven nonprofits and movements**, where the goal isn't revenue or product, but collective change. And where community isn't a strategy. It's the whole point.

Playbook 4: Nonprofits & Movements

For mission-driven organizations, community isn't a tactic. It's not an add-on or a "nice to have." It's **the engine of change.** Nonprofits, movements, and coalitions aren't trying to win market share. They're trying to **shift culture**, policy, behavior, sometimes all three. And for that kind of work to sustain, you need more than donations. More than headlines. You need people who show up, stay engaged, and bring others with them.

You need a community that is resilient, relational, and ready to move.

Unlike SaaS or creator ecosystems, where the value exchange is often direct (pay and receive, build and use), mission-driven communities operate on a more complex contract. People give time, money, and voice, not for personal gain. They do it because they believe the mission **matters more than their return.**

That makes trust even more fragile. And even more essential.

At the heart of every successful movement is **a sense of shared agency.** The feeling that *my voice, here, counts.* The reason that this isn't just an organization I support, it's **a movement I'm part of.**

That begins not with messaging, but with **mapping participation.** What are all the ways someone can belong? Is there a way to show up even if they can't donate? Is there a role even if they don't have credentials? Can they help onboard others, amplify campaigns, and organize local events?

The best communities don't just open the door; they offer **on-ramps.** Different speeds. Different shapes of engagement. All visible. All valued.

It's the difference between a newsletter subscriber and a volunteer. Between a passive follower and an organizer. Between liking a post and **owning the mission**.

And because movements often depend on volunteers, coordination becomes culture. Rituals, monthly calls, check-ins, and working groups help people feel the pulse. They see progress and feel a sense of proximity to change. And when the cause feels distant, these rhythms **close the gap between belief and action**.

In the next section, we'll explore how mission-driven communities maintain **momentum between moments**, how to stay active when the headlines fade, how to build infrastructure that holds together in quiet seasons, and how to use community as a **shock absorber for burnout**.

Because when the goal is change at scale, you don't just need voices. You need **staying power**.

Sustaining the Fire Between the Headlines

Movements burn bright in moments of crisis or change. A policy fight. A viral injustice. A public reckoning. Suddenly, attention floods in. Social feeds light up. Donations spike. Volunteers rush to help. The room fills with energy.

And then, silence.

The media cycle moves on. The urgency fades. And if there's no infrastructure beneath the surge, people drift. The moment passes without becoming a movement.

This is the gravity every mission-driven organization fights: the **drop-off after attention**, the slow erosion of momentum. And the answer isn't more campaigns or louder messaging. The answer is a **community that can breathe on its own**.

The most resilient nonprofits and causes treat the community not as an audience to be reactivated, but as **a body in motion**, with its metabolism. They design for seasons, times of action, and times of integration. They make space for people to show up at different tempos. And they create rituals that carry meaning **even when nothing's trending**.

That might be a monthly town hall. A gratitude ritual. A newsletter that doesn't just ask for donations but tells real stories from the field. It might be a WhatsApp thread for local organizers, a peer support space for activists, a reading circle that connects personal growth with political clarity.

These are not "high-engagement tactics." They are **anchors**, ways to tether people to one another when the outer winds are still.

Because staying involved in a mission is not just about the cause. It's about **staying connected to people who care about you just as much**.

And community is where that connection gets practiced, again and again, in moments small and large.

The second key to sustaining energy is **distributed ownership**. If the core team is the only one creating action, it will break. But if members can take initiative, organize an event, launch a campaign, and welcome newcomers, the movement becomes more than a center. It becomes **a network of nodes**, all reinforcing one another.

This is not chaos. It's intentional decentralization.

It requires trust, yes. Additionally, scaffolding toolkits, onboarding materials, and clear values are provided. Not to control, but to equip. When people know *how* to contribute and feel that their contribution matters, they show up more often, and they stay through the lulls. They don't wait to be told what to do. They **carry the mission forward in their language**.

In the final part of this playbook, we'll explore what happens when community becomes not just a tool for activism, but **a sanctuary from burnout**, a place where those doing the most challenging work also find the deepest replenishment.

Because in movements that last, people don't just fight together. They **heal together**, too.

A Place to Breathe: Community as Collective Care

The hardest part of working toward a cause isn't the strategy. It's the wear.

When you're up against injustice, systemic failure, slow policy, and limited resources, when every step forward feels like a battle, it's not uncommon for the most committed people to become the most depleted. Passion turns to fatigue. Hope starts to thin out. The cause remains, but the people behind it grow quiet. Or disappear.

This is why the most effective mission-driven communities don't just organize action. They **design for rest**.

Not performative wellness, not checkbox self-care. Real, community-powered replenishment. The kind that reminds people they are **more than the work they do**. That their value is not measured only in outcomes. That they are seen, held, and human.

In these communities, care isn't a side program. It's woven in.

A check-in circle where organizers speak without needing to perform strength. A moment at the end of every call to acknowledge what's heavy. A channel where someone can say, "I need to step back," and know they won't be shamed for it.

These are small gestures. But they change everything.

They create **a culture of return**. One where people don't burn out and vanish. They pause, heal, and re-enter because the community **remembers them as a whole**.

And that wholeness makes the mission stronger. Because when people feel safe, they take bigger risks. When they feel supported, they stay longer. When they feel held, they hold others. And over time, what you build is not just a movement, it's **a regenerative ecosystem of care and action**.

This is what the best mission-led communities teach us: that transformation requires endurance. And endurance requires **spaces that give back**.

They remind us that while campaigns may come and go, community **is what holds the thread across** seasons, leaders, setbacks, and wins. It's the container for continuity. For memory. For meaning.

And when the work feels too heavy to carry alone, the community says: *You don't have to.*

In the next section, we'll begin the final playbook of this chapter: for **open-source and developer-led ecosystems**, where community isn't just part of the value proposition. It *is* the product, the distribution, and the governance model all at once. Because when code is shared, **ownership must be, too.**

Playbook 5: Open Source

Most businesses build first, then invite others in. But in open-source ecosystems, the inverse is often true: the community exists **before the company**. Code is shared. People contribute. A culture forms. And only later does the question arise: *How do we support this at scale?*

This flips the script of traditional strategy. The moat is not proprietary IP. The product is not locked down. The leverage doesn't come from owning more; it comes from **being trusted to steward something shared**.

In that context, community isn't a marketing function. It's the **core infrastructure** of development, distribution, and long-term survival.

What makes this model powerful also makes it fragile. Because while open-source communities are self-organizing and highly generative, they are also deeply human. They require governance. Trust. Transparency. And above all, **mutual respect between builders and maintainers**.

Early on, it looks like momentum. Contributors fix bugs, add features, open issues, and debate standards. The project pulses with energy. But underneath the code, something subtler is taking shape: **a set of social contracts**.

How are decisions made? Who gets commit access? What happens when there's a disagreement over direction? These questions aren't technical; they're cultural. And the answers define whether the project remains a community or quietly becomes a company with a fan base.

The open-source playbook begins with a principle: **treat contributors like collaborators, not labor**.

That means visibility. It means credit. It means assuming good faith and building mechanisms to protect it. It also means clarity around roles, who's leading, who's guiding, and how others can participate meaningfully without needing to be "inside."

For developer-led communities, code is often the first contribution. But over time, others emerge writing docs, answering questions, triaging bugs, improving onboarding, and curating community tools. Each of these contributions has value. And when they're recognized as such, **the surface area of belonging expands**.

This is how developer ecosystems grow, not just by writing more code, but by building more **pathways into the work**.

In the next section, we'll explore how open-source projects balance **freedom with governance**, how they create structure without hierarchy, evolve direction without alienating contributors, and handle the inevitable tensions that arise when a few must lead something built by many. Because in open source, leadership is not authority. It's **earned trust, made visible**.

Governance Without the Guardrails Breaking

If code is the visible output of open-source projects, then **governance is the invisible scaffolding**. It's how decisions get made, how contributions are accepted, how disagreements are navigated. And it's what separates a thriving ecosystem from a charismatic founder bottleneck.

In the early stages, everything feels fluid, with a few core maintainers, a growing number of contributors, and informal processes. The vibe is collaborative, fast-moving, and even joyful. But as the project matures, so do the stakes; a key dependency breaks. A contributor burns out, and a disagreement over architecture balloons into a full-blown fork. And suddenly, everyone looks around and asks: *Who decides?*

This is the moment governance stops being optional. And the best projects prepare for it before they need it.

Good governance in open source doesn't mean bureaucracy. It means **shared clarity**. Who has merge rights? How are decisions documented? What are the escalation paths for disagreements? Is there a code of conduct, and does it guide behavior?

The answers to these questions aren't one-size-fits-all. Some communities adopt consensus models. Others use core teams or maintainership ladders. Still others create foundations or steering committees. But the common thread is this: the system works when it's **transparent, participatory, and trusted**.

Leadership, in these systems, isn't about asserting vision from the top. It's about **holding space**, for contributors, for disagreement, for evolution. The most effective open-source leaders understand their job is part coordinator, part mentor, part boundary-drawer. They don't need to win every argument. They need to ensure the project maintains **good faith**.

That means engaging in conflict with care, not suppressing disagreement, but **holding it in public** with humility and context. It means accepting that not every contributor will align on every goal, and that's okay. What matters is that the process for resolution is **clear, consistent, and culturally reinforced**.

Clarity is protective.

When people understand the rules, they're more likely to stay in the game. When expectations are explicit, contributors feel respected, even when their ideas aren't accepted. And when leadership is visible, but not dominant, communities scale **without fragility**.

As projects grow, another tension emerges: sustainability. Who pays for the infrastructure? Who funds the maintainers? How do you keep volunteers engaged when the work begins to feel like an obligation?

In the final part of this playbook, we'll explore how open-source communities address **long-term sustainability**, not just financially, but emotionally and structurally, so that the people who make the work possible aren't the ones sacrificed by its success. Because in the world of open code, **community health is system health**.

Sustaining the System: Funding, Burnout, and Long-Term Care

For all the power of open source, the speed, the distribution, the collective intelligence, there's a deep irony at its core: some of the world's most important software is **maintained by people working for free, at night, on the edge of burnout**.

A critical library. A foundational protocol. A dependency used by thousands of companies. And behind it, a single maintainer managing issues, fielding criticism, writing code, and wondering how long they can keep doing this.

This is the open-source sustainability crisis. And the only way through it is **community care by design**.

Sustainability starts with **recognition, not** just of contributors, but of contribution itself. Writing code is easy to see. But reviewing pull requests, moderating discussions, writing docs, and helping newcomers are the slow, often invisible forms of labor that hold ecosystems together.

Projects that survive the long haul find ways to **make that work visible**, through badges, shoutouts, contributor pages, and most importantly, **shared responsibility**. No one person should carry the full weight. If a maintainer disappears, the project shouldn't fall apart.

That means investing in process, not just code. Documenting what lives in people's heads. Onboarding new contributors with kindness, not gatekeeping. And rotating responsibility, so roles don't become traps.

Then comes the more challenging part: **funding**.

Open source has long relied on goodwill and volunteers. But goodwill doesn't pay rent. And while some employers support specific contributors, many do not. That's why more projects are turning to direct support models: GitHub Sponsors, Open Collective, grants, recurring donations, even commercial arms built around services, hosting, or integrations.

There's no one model. Some projects build nonprofits. Others start companies. Some remain decentralized but coordinate funding through foundations. What matters is **intentional structure**, knowing what kind of support you need, what trade-offs you're willing to accept, and how funding decisions will be made fairly.

And finally, sustainability means **emotional resilience**.

Maintainers need space to rest. To decline. To walk away if they need to. Communities that understand this create **a culture of permission**, where stepping back is not failure, but part of the rhythm of contribution. Where people can say, "I've done enough," and know they'll still be valued.

Because the health of an open-source project isn't just measured in commits. It's measured by **whether people still want to be there**.

When a developer ecosystem gets proper governance, clarity, recognition, and support, it becomes more than just a collection of repos. It becomes a place where people can do their best technical work **and be treated like full humans while doing it**.

That's the promise of open source at its best: Shared ownership. Shared care. Shared future.

In the next chapter, we'll step back from the playbooks and reflect on the patterns they reveal, and how to recognize when your community strategy is working... or where it's quietly going off track because good community strategy doesn't just help things grow. It helps them **endure**.

Chapter 17: When It Goes Wrong – Common Pitfalls

The Slow Unraveling

Not every community fails with fireworks.

There's no scandal. No dramatic implosion. No front-page takedown. More often, failure in community-led strategy is a quiet unraveling. It starts with a missed reply. A thread that goes unanswered. A core contributor who quietly drifts away. The weekly ritual that stops being weekly. The energy flattens, not overnight, but steadily, like air leaking from a tire.

And by the time someone notices, it's already too late. The community didn't break. It just **stopped feeling alive**.

That's the cruel trick of community failure: it rarely feels like failure until you're looking at it in the rearview. On the surface, everything seems fine. People are still logging in. Content still gets posted. Numbers hold steady. But the spark is gone. Participation becomes performance. Trust becomes transaction. And culture becomes something that used to happen here.

Every community-led strategy carries this risk. Not because community is fragile, but because it's **deeply human**.

And humans need more than systems. They need **signals of aliveness**, that someone's listening, that what they do matters, that this space still has a point of view. When those signals fade, no amount of tooling can replace them.

This chapter is not a catalog of horror stories. It's a mirror.

A place to reflect on the minor signs that something might be drifting off course. Because the earlier you notice the drift, the easier it is to **recover the center**.

We'll explore the most common pitfalls, the seductive but hollow moves that drain momentum. The scaling decisions that dilute the soul. The engagement tactics that mistake noise for depth. The role confusion leaves the community in a state of limbo, with no one sure who's steering the ship.

But first, we'll start with the most common, and most quietly corrosive, failure mode: **trying to grow something you haven't grounded**. Because before community is a channel, it's a choice. And if that choice isn't clear, the rest will never be.

Building Without Grounding

The idea was exciting. Maybe even urgent. *Let's build community.*

It felt like the right move. The market was shifting. The team was energized. The leadership wanted to "do something authentic." So, a Slack group was spun up. A Discord server. A "hub." A few ambassadors were invited, and a few emails were sent. The logo was added to the landing page.

And for a moment, it all seemed to hum. A couple of dozen people joined. There was chatter, emojis, and welcome threads. Someone asked a question. Someone else answered. You posted a prompt. You got some comments. You felt the buzz.

Then came the quiet.

Participation slowed. New members came in, looked around, and didn't post. Old ones didn't come back. The prompts started feeling like obligations. Engagement slipped. That early hum never came back. And you started asking: *Did we do something wrong?*

In a way, yes. You built the house before you understood who would live there.

This is the most common pitfall in community-led strategy: launching before grounding and creating a space without a story and designing for participation without knowing *why* people would choose to participate. Community becomes a checkbox, a feature, a tactic, but without clarity, it can't take root.

The truth is: community doesn't begin with platforms. It starts with **purpose**.

Before you build anything, you need to know who it's for, why it matters to them, and how you'll signal that **this is not just another room on the internet**. You need a point of view. A tension you're helping people navigate, a reason this space deserves to exist.

When that grounding isn't in place, even the best design won't stick. People won't know how to behave. They won't understand why they're here. And slowly, quietly, they'll disappear.

The fix isn't more engagement tactics. It's to stop, listen, and ask: *What does this community want to become?*

If you don't have a clear answer, the most strategic thing you can do isn't to post more. It's to pause. Reground. Rearticulate the "why" that will shape the "how." Because once the foundation is clear, even a small space can come alive again.

In the next section, we'll explore another typical failure pattern: **treating community like an audience**, where broadcasting replaces listening, and content strategy tries to stand in for human connection because the opposite of community is not absence. It's **performance without a relationship**.

Audience in Disguise

You're posting consistently. The content is good. People like it. They reshare. The numbers are solid. From a distance, it looks like momentum.

But something feels... off.

There's little depth in the replies. The conversation doesn't move unless you initiate it. Members aren't connecting with anyone except you. There's energy, but it's all one-way. When you stop posting, everything else stops, too.

This is the hidden trap of audience-thinking in community spaces.

It happens easily, especially for organizations that are used to broadcasting. The instinct is to share, to teach, to produce. And so when a community space is launched, it becomes just another **content channel**. Posts go out. Comments trickle in. Metrics are tracked. But the deeper pulse of a true community, mutuality, unpredictability, and belonging, is nowhere to be found.

What's missing isn't more content. It's **co-creation**.

In a community, value doesn't just flow outward. It moves in loops. A member asks a question, and another one answers. Someone shares a story, and others riff. One person offers a tool, and someone improves it. These exchanges can't be scheduled. They can only be **invited and trusted to happen**.

When the community is treated like the audience, members learn quickly: this isn't a place to show up as peers. It's a place to consume, react, maybe applaud. But never to shape. Never to own.

And slowly, the lurker rate rises. Participation drops. People stop checking in. It's not that they're bored. They **don't feel needed**.

To recover from this pattern, the shift isn't strategic. It's cultural.

You stop seeing yourself as the performer and begin seeing yourself as the host. Your content becomes a spark, not a script. You start highlighting member voices more than your own. You stop pushing for responses and start **curating moments that invite initiative**.

You also get curious: What would this community do if we stepped back? What kind of behavior would emerge if we weren't always at the center?

And then you make space for that to happen.

In the next section, we'll explore a third, more subtle failure: **over-scaling too soon**, when the drive for growth outpaces the maturity of the community, and the signal gets lost in the volume.

Because when everything gets bigger, you risk losing what made it matter in the first place.

Scaling Before the Center Holds

Growth feels like proof. More members. More messages. More motion. The numbers go up, and so does the pressure to keep them rising.

So, the invites get wider. The onboarding window gets shorter. The moderation thins. The culture dilutes. And slowly, imperceptibly at first, the shape of the space begins to change.

What was once coherent becomes crowded. What was once intimate becomes noisy. What was once yours... starts feeling like *just another forum*.

This is the cost of scaling too early. It doesn't break the system all at once; it **erodes the tone until it disappears**.

Many community-led strategies fail not because they lacked traction, but because they **couldn't sustain their growth**. They mistook an early signal for mature infrastructure. They assumed energy would carry the culture. But energy needs shape. And shape takes time to build.

At its best, a small community isn't a pilot. It's a **cultural laboratory**. A place to learn how people show up. How they talk. What they value. What rhythms support trust? What roles emerge? That early intimacy isn't just precious, it's **instructive**. It teaches you how to design for scale without losing soul.

But when you rush that stage, when you open the floodgates before the culture has roots, people don't grow it with you. They fill the space with what they know: memes, memes, memes. Shallow banter. Low-grade conflict. Engagement without coherence. And suddenly, your strategy becomes containment. You're not growing a community. You're **managing chaos**.

The irony is that many teams scale because they're afraid of missing a moment. The market's hot. The buzz is real. There's a window. But windows stay open longer than we think. And scaling before you're ready doesn't protect momentum. It just speeds up entropy.

So, the move is counterintuitive: slow down.

Resist the pressure to grow on schedule. Instead, deepen what already works. Codify your norms. Identify the behaviors worth amplifying. Train early stewards. Build the invisible architecture that can hold new energy. And **test your thresholds before you widen the doors because** scaling isn't just about more people. It's about more people who **feel the same way as the earliest ones**.

In the next section, we'll explore the consequences of **ambiguous ownership**, when no one knows who's responsible for the community, and it begins to drift, ungoverned and unsupported, because even the liveliest space needs someone to care for it. Otherwise, it stops being a community and becomes **just a platform**.

Who's Holding This?

Ask a team, "Who owns community here?" and you'll get a variety of answers. Marketing says they post the content. The product claims to listen to feedback. Support says they're in the forums. Leadership says everyone's responsible. But when you press, *who's accountable for the health, direction, and culture of this space?* The air gets thin.

This is the quiet crisis of ownership.

When no one holds the center of a community, the consequences don't manifest as chaos. They show up as **slow abandonment**. Unanswered questions. Unmoderated threads. New members are unsure where to go. Core members are doing unpaid labor because no one else is paying attention.

And even when someone does feel responsible, they're often under-resourced, isolated, or stretched thin across functions. They're expected to be strategists, therapists, social media managers, and crisis responders, all while proving ROI on a spreadsheet.

Without clear ownership, the community becomes a liminal space, visible and valued, yet structurally unsupported.

It starts to slide into organizational orphanhood. Everyone agrees it matters. No one funds it adequately. Everyone wants outcomes. No one invests in care.

To fix this, you don't just assign a name. You **build a mandate**.

That means defining what community is *for* in your organization. Is it a driver of product insight? A brand amplifier? A member success channel? A revenue stream? A pipeline for talent? A strategic differentiator? You don't need a single answer; you need a primary one, along with a shared understanding of how other functions integrate.

Then you fund it like you mean it. That means more than headcount. It means access to leadership, clear KPIs, room to experiment, and internal cultural support. A valid owner can't just steward the space; they must **advocate for it internally**, across teams, and up the ladder.

Sometimes the fix isn't one person. It's a **cross-functional structure**. A community guild. A steering circle. A shared set of roles and rhythms that hold the work without putting it all on one overwhelmed lead.

What matters most is that the community knows: *someone is tending this space.* That presence alone builds safety. And safety builds participation.

In the next section, we'll explore a final, often painful failure mode: **when the soul gets lost**, when a community scales, formalizes, and professionalizes to the point that the magic evaporates.

Because the opposite of toxicity isn't neutrality, it's **aliveness**.

The Soul Slips Out

It's still active. The numbers are substantial. The brand has polish. The tone is professional. Everything's working. And yet, it doesn't feel like it used to.

The conversations are clean, but careful. The questions are answered, but briefly. The events run on time. The threads stay civil. The metrics remain up. And still, something essential is missing.

It's the warmth. The weirdness. The spark.

What once felt like a place now feels like a service. What once felt like *ours* now feels like *theirs*. And no one can quite name when it happened.

This is the final and most heartbreaking pitfall: **the loss of soul**.

It doesn't come from malice or mismanagement. It comes from success. From structure. From the well-meaning instinct to professionalize, scale, and systematize. And one day, you realize: you've built something smooth, efficient, and hollow.

The original members started logging in less. Newer members never quite attach. The content is good, but it lacks energy. The calls are organized, but no one lingers afterward. The community hasn't failed. It has simply **flattened**.

And often, the instinct is to fix it with programming. More events. More channels. More prompts. But the soul doesn't respond to quantity. It responds to **presence**. And presence, at scale, takes intention.

Sometimes, it's as simple as a story.

A reintroduction to the purpose of the space. A reminder of the first conversation that sparked it all. A celebration of a member who went above and beyond. A visible return to what made this feel like *a place where I could be me.*

Sometimes, it's the subtle refusal to sanitize. Letting messiness in. Letting humor, imperfection, and play breathe again. Trusting that culture can be professional *without becoming cold.*

And sometimes, it's stepping back, not from the work, but from the systems and creating unstructured space and letting members lead, and remembering that the deepest signal of community health isn't efficiency. It's aliveness.

Aliveness has texture. It's not always polite. Not always productive. But it's **felt.** And that feeling is what makes people return, even when they're busy, even when they're burned out, even when they're on the edge of leaving it all behind.

Because in a world full of polished platforms and templated conversations, to feel something real is rare. And when you lose that, no number can replace it.

The lesson is not to resist structure. It's a design structure that **protects aliveness**, not replaces it. That elevates participation over programming.

Because in the end, no one joins a community for perfect execution. They participate in the magic. And they stay for the meaning.

In the next and final chapter, we'll look forward to what comes next, not just for individual communities, but for the

future of community-led strategy itself. The trends, the tensions, and the transformations are just beginning to emerge.

Because if the past decade was about recognizing the power of community, the next will be about **learning to lead with it.**

Chapter 18: The Future of Community-Led Strategy

The Shape of What's Coming

It's becoming harder to tell where organizations end and communities begin.

Ten years ago, the community lived on the margins, relegated to marketing or support roles, which involved managing forums, answering tickets, and occasionally hosting events. But now, it's moved closer to the center. Product teams build with communities. Hiring pipelines run through them. Brand strategy draws its tone from them. Investors listen to what they're saying. Culture itself takes cues from how communities behave.

The shift didn't come from theory. It came from the unmistakable clarity that **people trust people more than institutions**. That trust doesn't scale the same way infrastructure does. And that the places we return to, online, in person, or hybrid, are the ones where we feel seen, not sold to.

We're at a moment where community isn't just a strategic asset. It's **an organizing principle**.

But as with all things that rise quickly, this momentum brings complexity. Growth creates pressure. New tools create noise. And the more that community becomes a business function, the more it risks losing what made it so powerful in the first place.

Still, something more profound is forming beneath the surface, a new kind of architecture, not just for connection, but for **how organizations define themselves through the people who surround them**.

Community is no longer confined to a platform or product. It is becoming a **strategic philosophy**: a way of structuring participation, distributing ownership, and adapting to change without losing cohesion. The most forward-thinking teams aren't just asking how to build community, they're asking how to **build *with* community** from the start.

This new phase won't be about launching spaces or tracking engagement. It will be about how organizations design systems that are porous, relational, and co-owned. Where culture isn't just branded, but embodied. Where users become contributors. Where customers become collaborators. Where the line between internal and external blurs into a shared center of gravity.

In the next section, we'll explore three powerful forces already reshaping the future of community-led strategy: the rise of **AI as mediator**, the emergence of **decentralized models of belonging**, and the growing urgency for **repair-centered spaces** in a fragmented, exhausted world.

This is not a trend forecast. It's a sketch of a new foundation being laid, quietly, and by many hands.

Intelligence at the Edges

The arrival of AI into the fabric of community is less dramatic than some predicted, but more intimate than anyone expected.

At first, it was surface level: more intelligent bots, better moderation, tools that could parse sentiment or summarize threads. Useful, yes. But impersonal. It seemed that AI would exist at the edges, automating repetitive tasks so humans could focus on meaningful connections.

That boundary hasn't held.

AI is now not just managing information but helping shape the context of interaction. It suggests introductions. It surfaces latent themes. It nudges quiet members at just the right time. It helps people feel seen, even before another human has typed a reply. In some communities, it even begins the conversation.

This isn't inherently a problem. In many cases, it's a relief. The cognitive load of stewardship can be overwhelming. And when AI steps in with care, well-trained, transparent, contextually aware, it can preserve the energy that community builders need to focus on depth, not maintenance.

But the questions start to shift. What happens when a member's most frequent and helpful interaction is with a model? When will AI become the first and most available touchpoint? When you can't always tell which welcome message was written by a human hand and which one was suggested, prefilled, or generated?

These aren't dystopian concerns. They're present-day tensions. And they force a deeper inquiry, not just about what AI can do for the community, but **what it should be trusted to do**.

Because the core of community is not speed or scale, it's care.

And care doesn't always look like efficiency. Sometimes it seems like silence held just long enough for someone else to step in. Sometimes it resembles the long, uneven rhythm of a real conversation, awkward, unoptimized, and full of nuance. Sometimes it seems like choosing *not* to fill a gap, so a human can notice it and respond in kind.

As AI becomes more integrated into community systems, the question won't be whether it can replicate empathy. The question is whether our systems can be designed to **amplify humanity without erasing it**.

In the best-case version, AI becomes a kind of infrastructure, not visible, not leading, but quietly supporting the emotional labor of connection. It helps us notice, remember, and respond. It extends our reach without compromising our voice. And it returns something we often lose to overwhelm, **attention**.

In the next section, we'll explore a parallel evolution: **the rise of decentralized belonging**, how web3, federated models, and portable identity are breaking the idea that community must be bound to a platform at all.

What happens when people carry their community with them, instead of being asked to join someone else's?

Belonging Without Borders

Community used to mean place. A town. A school. A forum. A shared URL where people gathered and returned. But increasingly, the center of gravity is shifting, not toward a location, but toward the individual.

People don't join platforms anymore. They **join people**. And increasingly, they expect to take their identity with them.

The rise of web3 models, decentralized identity, and federated infrastructure has accelerated this shift, but it didn't start there. It began the moment people realized that most online communities weren't theirs. The moment they saw a platform pivot and take everything with it. The moment the algorithm changed, suddenly no one could reach each other.

That's when the idea of portable belonging began to matter. The idea that your contributions, your relationships, your status in a space shouldn't be locked behind someone else's login screen. That identity in a community shouldn't reset when you move platforms. That your reputation should travel with you, not as a product to monetize, but as a record of **participation that mattered**.

What's emerging now is not a single new platform, but **a new posture toward platforms**.

In this next era, communities are less about owning a space and more about **weaving a network**. They'll move across tools. Across protocols. Across time zones and interfaces. The community will thrive in the layer of trust between people, not in the software that merely holds their words.

For organizations, this demands a reframing. If you can no longer count on "hosting" people indefinitely, how do you support them meaningfully? How do you create shared language, norms, and memory when the space itself is fluid?

You design for continuity without control.

You stop anchoring everything to a platform and begin anchoring it to **ritual, story, and shared values**. You design artifacts that can move, code, create zines, create knowledge bases, and create guides. You build infrastructure that doesn't collapse if a tool sunsets. And you learn to see "leaving" not as a loss, but as **circulation**, a healthy sign of interconnected ecosystems.

This is where community becomes **movement**. Not in the political sense, necessarily, but in the energetic one. It moves because it's not tied to a building. It breathes, because no one owns the air.

And when the community moves like this, the question isn't how many members you have. It's **how far your relationships travel**.

In the final section of this chapter, we'll explore a more profound shift already underway: the rise of **repair-centered community spaces**, spaces not just for growth, but for reckoning, restoration, and reinvention.

Because if the future of community-led strategy is about more than reach, it must also be about **return**.

The Future Is for Repair

Beneath the talk of tools and trends, something quieter is happening in community spaces. Something less marketable, but more urgent.

People are arriving not just to connect, but to recover. To mend what's been frayed by years of digital overload, social fragmentation, and institutional collapse. To find some place, any place, that feels human enough to stay.

This isn't the future community strategy that was planned. But it may be the one that matters most.

In spaces where belonging is real, something else becomes possible: **repair**. Not as a metaphor. Not as an aesthetic. But as an act. A space where people don't need to be impressive, optimized, or "on-brand." Where they can show up in uncertainty and still be held in clarity.

The best communities of the future won't just scale, they'll **soften**. They'll become places where grief has room, where disconnection isn't met with punishment, but patience, where disagreement is allowed to live without rupture. Where the whole self, not just the strategic self, is welcome.

This doesn't mean abandoning outcomes or abandoning ambition. It means remembering that strategy without care is cold. If you want people to stay, you have to be willing to hold more than their enthusiasm. You have to be able to keep their weariness, too.

Community strategy, in this next era, will be as much about architecture as it is about **attunement**.

Are we designing spaces that can metabolize conflict, not avoid it? Can we support leaders without asking them to be invulnerable? Can we create rituals that acknowledge the weight people are carrying, not just what we hope they'll produce?

These are not soft questions. They're strategic ones. Because when community becomes a place of repair, it becomes the one thing people won't churn from. It becomes a space they return to, not out of obligation, but out of **recognition**.

They return because it reminds them of something they've forgotten, and they want to address it as soon as possible, as it provides a way to move forward.

This is where community-led strategy goes next, not into bigger launches or more intelligent automation, but into **deeper responsibility**.

To each other. To the work. To the world, we're shaping the way we gather. Because the future of community isn't just about connection, it's about what we're willing to do with that connection, together.

Appendix A: The Community-Led Strategy Canvas

Framing the Canvas

Strategy is easy to overthink and hard to practice, especially when it comes to community.

The metrics are messier. The outcomes unfold slowly. The work requires equal parts systems thinking and emotional intelligence. And most of all, it requires that we hold space, for contradiction, for complexity, for people who don't fit neatly into business categories.

That's why this canvas exists.

Not to reduce the community to a template, but to give form to the essential decisions that shape it. To make visible the relationships between values, goals, behaviors, and design. To help you hold all the moving pieces in one place, ask: *What are we building here? And why?*

The canvas has seven parts. You don't need to complete them in order. You don't need to finish them all at once. What matters is how they **interact**, how a decision in one part affects the shape of the others. The goal isn't completion. It's coherence.

At the heart of the canvas is a tension: you're building something emergent, but you still need direction. You're inviting people in, but you need boundaries. You're measuring growth, but you can't force intimacy. This canvas is where you wrestle with those tensions, honestly, and without the need for perfect answers.

The following section will walk through each segment of the canvas, in narrative form, what it asks, why it matters, and how to approach it without flattening your community into a content calendar or an onboarding funnel.

This is not a formula. It's a framework for thinking with clarity and care.

Purpose – The Center of Gravity

Everything in the community starts with purpose. Not the surface-level goals. Not the campaign. Not the launch event. But the **deep why**, the reason this community should exist at all.

Without purpose, a community becomes just another content stream. Just another forum. Just another room where people say hello, then quietly disappear.

But when the purpose is clear, when it is felt, not just stated, people begin to organize themselves around it. They feel it in the tone of a welcome message. In the kinds of questions that get asked. In what's celebrated and what isn't. They don't just join the space. They begin to **inhabit it**.

So, the question isn't "What's the purpose of this community? "It's: *What is this community in service of?*

Is it helping people learn a craft they care about? Is it creating pace for mutual aid or advocacy? Is it about identity and the power of being seen by others like you? Is it about shaping the future of a product or movement? Is it about healing, remembering, reimagining?

You don't need a slogan. You need a **point of view**, one strong enough to guide decisions, and generous enough to let people find their place inside it.

When you name your purpose clearly, everything else starts to click. It becomes easier to say no. Easier to welcome people who are aligned. Easier to recognize when the work is drifting off course.

If you're not sure what your community's purpose is yet, start with stories. Ask yourself: when was the moment you knew this needed to exist? Who showed up first, and why? What problem or hunger brought them to you?

Let the answers shape your center, for it will hold everything else.

In the next section, we'll explore the second piece of the canvas: **People**, who the community is for, how they show up, and what they're looking for when they arrive.

People – Who This Is For

Strategy becomes real when you stop building for *everyone* and start building for **someone**.

Communities aren't made of personas. They're made of people. Real ones, with contradictions and constraints, with dreams that don't fit neatly into business models, and with histories that shape how they show up.

So, the question isn't "Who is our audience?" It's deeper: Who are we inviting into this space? And what are they carrying with them when they arrive?

Too many communities try to serve too broad a swath: "creatives," "founders," "users," "humans who care." But when a community speaks to everyone, it rarely resonates deeply with anyone. People don't join spaces because they feel generic. They participate because they think **that**, like this place, it understands something about their life they didn't have words for yet.

Start with one real person. Picture them. Not the idealized version, the actual one. What are they navigating right now? What are they frustrated with? Where are they stuck? What do they long for that's hard to name? Who do they wish they had around them?

Build from there.

A useful lens here is *motivation*. Not just "why would they join?", but what are they hoping this space will help them become? Are they looking to sharpen a skill? To be inspired? To be seen? To escape isolation? To take action? To make meaning?

These aren't tactical preferences. They're **emotional drivers**. And when you understand those, you can shape your design around them, not just your onboarding flow, but your tone, your rituals, your programming, your norms.

You can also build for **divergence**: not all members will want the same thing, and that's okay. Some may come to contribute. Others to learn. Others to watch quietly from the edges. Your job isn't to force uniformity. It's to make space for different forms of belonging, without losing the thread that holds them together.

And don't forget you are one of the people, too. Your role, your needs, your boundaries, your vision, those are part of the relational ecosystem. If you prioritize the needs of others over your own, the strategy may look good on paper but feel unsustainable in practice.

Once you truly understand the people, you stop guessing. You stop designing for conversion and start planning for **continuity**. And the work begins to shift from *how do we grow this? How can we deepen it to attract more of the right people?*

In the next section, we'll explore the third piece of the canvas: **Participation**, how people show up, what roles they take on, and how you turn passive presence into meaningful co-creation.

Participation – Turning Presence Into Belonging

It's one thing to have people show up. It's another for them to **participate in a way that matters** to them and the community.

Participation isn't a metric. It's a relationship. It reflects the invisible question every member carries with them into the space: *Is there something meaningful for me to do here?*

Not just a task. A **role**. A sense that their presence makes a difference. That their contributions shift the shape of the space, even a little. That there is room for them not only to consume, but to shape.

Designing for participation begins with possibility. What are the natural ways people might engage, based on your purpose and who they are? Not every community needs contributors to be creators. Some need conversation. Some need stewardship. Some need reflection. Some need amplification. Some people need others to hold space for them to feel welcome.

It also requires clarity. If people are waiting for permission or unsure of the "rules," they won't step in. But when you signal what's expected, what's encouraged, and what's possible, you reduce friction. You create a path. You tell them: *this isn't just a place to watch. It's a place to participate.*

Roles often emerge organically: greeters, guides, provocateurs, caretakers, synthesizers, documenters. You don't need to invent all these roles in advance. You need to **notice**

them when they appear and build structures that let them grow without burning out.

One mistake many communities make is trying to incentivize participation with rewards, badges, points, and status markers. These tools can be helpful, but only when they reflect something **already meaningful**. If the structure exists only to gamify behavior, it won't stick. But if it reveals and honors what people care about, it deepens commitment.

It's also important to accept that participation is not always visible. Lurking isn't failure; it's a form of listening. And often, those on the edge are the ones most profoundly shaped by the culture. Design for them, too. Let them feel that even in silence, they're still part of the fabric.

Ultimately, participation is not about quantity. It's about **aliveness**. Do people feel their presence matters? Do they leave more energized than when they arrived? Do they return not because they have to, but because the space *does something for them*, and maybe, through them?

In the next section, we'll explore the fourth element of the canvas: **Pathways**, how participation evolves, how members grow, and how you create momentum without pressure.

Pathways – Designing for Growth Without Force

In healthy communities, people change. They arrive curious, unsure, maybe tentative. They stay, and something shifts. They start to contribute. They take a small risk. They offer help. They step into a role. Sometimes they lead.

This doesn't happen because someone assigned a journey to them. It occurs because the space is designed to **make growth visible and available**, without pressure, but with possibility.

Pathways are the connective tissue between participation and potential. They answer the question: *Once someone is here, what becomes possible for them?*

There's no universal map. Pathways don't need to look like a funnel or a ladder. They often move in loops, pauses, and sideways turns. But the community builder's job is to **notice the patterns of evolution** and to support them gently.

Start by understanding your members' emotional arcs. What do they need when they arrive? What tends to unlock their first contribution? What shifts when they feel seen? When do they stall? When do they rise into greater ownership?

Then, design for those thresholds. Not with pressure, but with **invitations**. Maybe it's a welcome ritual that gently encourages expression. Perhaps it's a moment when you ask someone to co-host. Maybe it's a lightweight ask that turns a lurker into a participant. Perhaps it's a mentorship role offered at just the right time.

The goal isn't to push people up a hierarchy. It's to create **openings**. And those openings become momentum, because when someone crosses a threshold and is affirmed, it's not just their behavior that changes. It's their identity. They begin to think: *I belong here. I matter here. I can help shape this.*

Importantly, you also need to make it easy to pause, as people's energy changes. Life interrupts. If you don't normalize withdrawal, you create shame. If you don't honor returns, you limit resilience. A well-designed community isn't just good at activation. It's good at **re-entry**.

And finally, pathways are not just for members. They're for you. You grow, too, in skill, in insight, in capacity. The best community strategies aren't fixed blueprints. They're **learning ecosystems**, where growth is mutual.

In the next section, we'll explore the fifth layer of the canvas: **Place**, how the design of the environment (physical, digital, or hybrid) shapes behavior, emotion, and culture.

Place – Making Space Feel Like Something

Place isn't just where community happens. It's how it happens.

Whether digital or physical, synchronous or asynchronous, open or private, every space carries signals. It tells people how to behave, how to feel, and whether they're truly welcome.

Too often, we think of place as a platform choice. Do we use Slack or Discord? A Facebook group? A custom app? But these questions, while practical, miss the deeper one: *What kind of atmosphere are we trying to create? And what space will best support that feeling?*

Space is emotional architecture. A dark-mode forum with complex threads encourages a different energy than a real-time chat room with GIFs flying. A living document open for comment feels different from a broadcast webinar. A small in-person meetup in a café holds different possibilities than a 5,000-person conference hall.

Designing a place is about alignment. What does your purpose call for? What do your people naturally gravitate toward? What kind of participation are you hoping to invite? Quiet reflection? Fast feedback? Casual intimacy? Structured learning?

And once chosen, how is that space tended?

The best community spaces feel *held*. Not overdesigned, not cluttered with tabs and widgets, but cared for. They have rhythm and structure. Clear entry points. Thoughtful moderation. They're not just places to go; they're places to **return to**.

This is especially important for digital communities, where the default is entropy. Without care, tools become graveyards. But with the right design, a digital space can feel as emotionally textured as a room with candles and couches.

You also need to make the place porous. If everything happens in one locked-down channel or silo, you limit discovery. But if you open everything, you risk dilution. The balance is subtle: enough openness to welcome the right people in, enough boundaries to let safety and culture root deeply.

And don't forget the physical layer. Even in primarily digital communities, there are moments when gathering offline can deepen the relational bonds in ways nothing else can. A dinner. A retreat. A serendipitous meetup. These aren't just perks. They're **rituals of embodiment**, reminders that behind every handle is a human.

When a place is well-designed, people don't just consume or perform. They **relax**. They trust the space. They find their rhythm inside it. And that rhythm is the foundation for everything else that will grow.

In the next section, we'll move into the sixth element of the canvas: **Pace**, the tempo of your community, and how time, cadence, and rhythm shape energy, trust, and longevity.

Pace – Finding the Right Rhythm

Not everything needs to move fast, especially not the community.

Many of the most meaningful communities operate at a slower, more deliberate pace. One that respects people's attention, honors their energy, and creates time for trust to grow, not just activity to spike.

Pace is more than a scheduling decision. It's the emotional tempo of your community. The cadence that governs not just what happens, but how it feels when it does.

Are things happening daily, weekly, or quarterly? Is the space always buzzing, or are there seasons of quiet? Are people expected to respond in real-time, or can they settle in, read, reflect, and return on their own time?

Each of these choices communicates values. A weekly ritual says, *We value rhythm.* A pop-up challenge says, *We value bursts of energy.* A long-form conversation says, *We value depth over speed.* A seasonal gathering says, *We understand people need rest.*

The danger isn't in choosing the wrong pace. It's in **not choosing at all**. Without intentionality, most communities default to urgency, constant activity, constant prompts, and constant performance. But urgency can't sustain trust. It burns bright, then burns out.

By contrast, thoughtful pacing lets you design for **coherence over time**. You can build cycles that include activation and integration, events followed by reflection. Sprints balanced with stillness. When the rhythm is precise, members don't worry about missing something; they know the beat will come back around.

You also build space for **absence without guilt**. When people know the community will still be there, alive, intact, welcoming, they can step away and return without shame. And that freedom increases their commitment, not their distance.

Some communities even experiment with intentional pauses: quiet months, reflection periods, sabbaticals from programming. These aren't signs of inactivity. They're signs of **integrity**. They reflect a commitment to people's actual capacities, not idealized engagement curves.

Ultimately, pace is a tool for health. Because when time is honored, people feel honored. And when they feel honored, they return, not just often, but fully.

In the final section of this appendix, we'll explore the seventh and anchoring element: **Proof**, how you know what's working, what matters, and what impact your community is having.

Proof – Knowing What Matters

The pressure to prove the community's value is real.

Leaders want dashboards. Stakeholders want outcomes. The business wants a story with numbers attached. And as a community builder, you're often caught between the aliveness of the work and the need to make that aliveness legible to others.

But value in the community doesn't always show up as data. Sometimes it shows up as energy. As trust. As a conversation that would never have happened anywhere else. There's a moment when someone says, "This space changed the way I see myself."

Still, strategy requires reflection. We need to understand what's working, not just to justify our efforts, but to honor and deepen them.

That's where proof comes in.

Proof is not just about measurement. It's about **meaning-making**. It's the process of surfacing what matters, how it moves, and what shifts as a result of the space you've created.

Yes, that can include quantitative metrics: activation, retention, contribution, net promoter scores, and participation curves. But it must also include qualitative insight: testimonials, stories, emergent patterns, quiet transformations that data might miss.

The key is **coherence** between what you say you value and what you choose to track.

If your purpose is about peer-to-peer learning, show how many connections have formed. If your aim is member transformation, gather stories of change. If you're cultivating leadership, surface the pathways people are walking and the roles they're stepping into.

And importantly, share your proof with the community, not just the company. Let people see their impact reflected to them. Celebrate what's growing. Name what's shifted. Invite members into the act of sense-making. This turns measurement into **recognition**.

And recognition is not just rewarding. It's reinforcing. It reminds people that their time here matters. That the culture they're shaping is authentic. That the work they're doing, visible or not, is seen and valued.

When proof is treated this way, it stops being a burden. It becomes a ritual. A mirror. A way of saying: *This is who we are, and this is what we're building, together.*

Appendix B: Case Studies

Case Study 1: Notion

When Notion first began to gain traction, it wasn't because of a brilliant ad campaign. It wasn't because of slick sales funnels or viral stunts. It was because people started **building with it**, and then they began discussing their creations.

The early Notion user wasn't just a note-taker. They were a tinkerer. A document architect. Someone who looked at a blank workspace and saw potential. And instead of keeping that creativity to themselves, they shared it. Public templates. Use cases. Workflows. They taught others how to think in blocks.

Notion noticed. But rather than rushing to formalize or monetize the community, they did something more subtle. They **celebrated it**. Amplified it. Made space for it to grow on its terms.

They invited power users into early access programs, not just as a perk, but as a way to **co-design the future** of the product. They shared roadmaps, not as a performance metric, but as a conversation. And they made it easy for people to share their creations, with lightweight tools, curated directories, and just enough recognition to feel seen without being used.

As the community grew, so did its diversity. Designers used it to manage portfolios. Educators used it to build open syllabi. Startup founders ran entire companies inside it. Each use case became a **signal**, attracting others with similar needs and creativity.

Notion didn't create all these paths. They made a **canvas for them to emerge**.

What's strategic about Notion's community isn't just its size or enthusiasm. It's how the company understood its role, not as the center of attention, but as **a steward of possibility**. The platform became a stage. The community became the playwrights, actors, and directors.

And as that ecosystem matured, Notion began investing more deliberately: local ambassador programs, community-curated content, international user groups. But all of it was built on a foundation of **trust and autonomy**, the understanding that the most valuable community activity is often the kind you couldn't have scripted if you tried.

If Notion teaches us anything, it's this: when your product invites creation, your community will invite connection. But only if you let them build and then get out of the way.

Case Study 2: Duolingo – When the Game Becomes Gathering

At first glance, Duolingo doesn't look like a community. It seems like a well-designed app. A language-learning tool. A gamified system of streaks, lessons, XP points, and friendly reminders from a neon green owl.

But linger for a few weeks, especially as your streak stretches on, and something more begins to take shape.

People don't just use Duolingo. They identify with it. They talk about it. They form streak groups and message each other when one of them is about to fall off. They create memes, inside jokes, and elaborate stories around Duo the owl. They don't just learn *in* Duolingo. They begin to **belong to it**.

That shift, from a product with users to a space with members, didn't happen by accident. It happened because Duolingo did something deceptively simple: it **invited play**.

From the start, Duolingo's design leaned into the psychology of participation. Not just extrinsic motivation, like badges and leaderboards, but *micro-rituals* that created emotional attachment. The daily streak became a kind of identity. Skipping a lesson didn't just risk your progress; it felt like breaking a promise to yourself and others tracking alongside you.

But Duolingo didn't stop at gamification. They began listening. They observed how people discussed the app online, noting the emergence of humor and the formation of cultural micro-movements around its voice and presence. Then they **leaned in**.

They turned Duo into a character. Not just a logo, but a cheeky, emotionally expressive mascot with a tone that blended encouragement and chaos. They let the community co-create that voice, then *canonized it* through social media, notifications, and even product copy.

More importantly, they began to support emergent communities around the edges. Language challenge groups. Subreddits. Discord servers. Instead of trying to centralize everything, Duolingo allowed **distributed identity** to flourish. People could form whatever kind of relationship they wanted, with the product, with each other, with the process of learning itself.

In doing so, they achieved something most ed-tech platforms struggle to touch: **joy.** Not just learning outcomes, but cultural presence. Not just engagement, but *emotion.*

What Duolingo proves is that community doesn't always need forums or hosts or ambassadors. Sometimes it grows in the margins, in jokes, habits, rituals, and the sense that you're part of something a little bigger than your daily practice. Something that reflects you to yourself with just enough delight to make you want to keep going.

And once that connection is made, it sticks. Not just because of the features. Because of the **feeling.**

Case Study 3: Figma – Community as Creative Commons

Figma didn't set out to build a community. It set out to reimagine how people design together.

From its earliest days, Figma was built on a radical proposition: design could be real-time, multiplayer, and browser-based. That technical shift, what it enabled, was the beginning of everything else. By removing friction from collaboration, you create a new kind of **creative proximity**.

Designers who once shared static files could now co-create in real time. Comments could live directly on the canvas. Work didn't need to be handed off; it could be co-shaped. And that simple ability to *see each other working* became the cultural heartbeat of the product.

What followed wasn't just adoption. It was an **emergence**.

Design systems began to take shape publicly. Teams opened up templates, workshops, and prototypes to the broader world. People didn't just learn Figma, they started teaching it, remixing it, building libraries and plugins. Suddenly, a tool for product design became a **platform for creative generosity**.

Figma recognized this quickly. Instead of locking the ecosystem down, they opened it wider. The Figma Community platform was launched, not as a branding tool, but as a **distribution network for shared imagination**. Anyone could publish their work. Anyone could copy, adapt, or remix.

This is where Figma's community strategy took root: in the decision to build *with* its users, not just *for* them.

They amplified the creators. Not just big agencies, but independent educators, toolmakers, niche voices. They held community events, both global and local, but kept the tone practical, open, and lightly playful. No one was too junior to contribute. No one is too senior to learn.

And in parallel, they kept their product strategy aligned. Every central feature leaned into **visibility, collaboration, and open expression**. When Figma launched, it wasn't just a new canvas; it was a new way for people to think together, sketch messily, and co-invent in real time.

Figma's strength has never just been its functionality. It's been its ability to reflect a particular kind of creative ethos: generous, collaborative, iterative. A philosophy that the community already held, but that Figma gave **a home and a language**.

Now, when people think of design collaboration, they often think of *Figma* first. But more importantly, when they think of *creative community*, Figma is in the conversation, not because it claimed that space, but because it consistently **invited others to help build it**.

What this case makes clear is that the most vibrant communities don't grow from brand mandates. They grow from product truths. From tools that make participation feel natural. From platforms that invite generosity. From companies willing to listen, then lift.

Case Study 4: Glossier – Customers as Culture-Makers

When Glossier entered the beauty world, it didn't arrive with a marketing blitz or a celebrity endorsement. It came with a blog.

Into The Gloss, the blog Emily Weiss launched before the brand existed, was a space to listen. It featured interviews, product reviews, behind-the-scenes routines, written not by marketers, but in the voice of the curious insider. It asked readers questions. It invited feedback. It published comments. And in doing so, it created something rare in beauty: a space where consumers felt *spoken with*, not *spoken at*.

This wasn't content as promotion. It was content as **community soil**.

By the time Glossier launched its first products, there was already a relationship in place. Not a traditional sales funnel, but a network of people who felt like they'd been part of the process all along. And that feeling didn't fade. It intensified.

Glossier's early strategy revolved around two powerful ideas: **intimacy and invitation**.

The intimacy came from the tone, which was direct, unfiltered, and lightly playful, and deeply attuned to how real people talk about beauty. The invitation came from Structure: customers were invited to test products, weigh in on development, and even suggest names. The line between brand and buyer blurred, not by accident, but by design.

Glossier didn't build a community around its product. It **built a product inside its community**.

That feedback loop, between the company and its most engaged members, became a strategic advantage. Glossier wasn't just fast to market. It was culturally resonant because it was *already in conversation* with the people it hoped to serve.

As the brand grew, it continued to invest in those relationships. Pop-ups weren't just sales events; they were gatherings. Instagram wasn't just a marketing channel; it was a living mood board where comments turned into product cues. The DMs weren't ignored. They were answered, often personally, often warmly.

Of course, like many companies that rise quickly on community energy, Glossier faced challenges. Growth introduced new layers, scale, retail complexity, and public scrutiny. The intimacy became harder to maintain. The community model, once fluid, strained under the weight of mainstream success.

But the foundational insight remains that when customers help shape the soul of the brand, they don't just buy. They **belong**. And that belonging isn't a loyalty program. It's a felt relationship. One that survives product cycles, pivots, and even periods of silence, so long as the original *respect* is preserved.

Glossier taught the beauty industry that influence isn't always top-down. It can start in the comments. In a question. In a story shared at the right time, in the right tone, with the right intention.

It taught all of us that community isn't an add-on. Sometimes, it's the **source code**.

Case Study 5: Stripe – Infrastructure With Culture

Stripe doesn't sell community. It sells payment infrastructure. Apis. Documentation. Financial plumbing.

But beneath that technical surface, Stripe has cultivated something rare: a sense of cultural alignment so strong that developers, founders, and operators talk about Stripe not just as a service, but as a *standard*, a platform they want to build with, and often, build around.

This didn't come from flashy community programs or gamified forums. It came from **intellectual generosity**, **precision of voice**, and a long-term commitment to **serving people who build things**.

From the beginning, Stripe did things differently. Its documentation wasn't just clear, it was *elegant*. The onboarding wasn't just fast; it felt like it understood the mental model of a developer before they asked the question. This wasn't marketing. It was **empathy, expressed through craft**.

That same posture showed up in how Stripe communicated with the world. Instead of plastering ads, they published essays. Thoughtful, technically literate, often philosophical in tone. Stripe understood that its audience, engineers, product thinkers, and early-stage founders valued ideas. So, they offered them. Freely. Without pandering.

And when Stripe began building outward, it didn't start with a community manager. It started with **ecosystem thinking**.

The company quietly supported meetups. It partnered with early-stage founders. It invested in developer tools that enhanced the performance of other products. It created Stripe Atlas, a platform to help global entrepreneurs incorporate and get banking access in the U.S., not as a revenue driver, but as **a strategic gesture of belief in the builder economy**.

All of this created what looked, from the outside, like a developer community. But it wasn't "run" by Stripe. It was **rooted** in the trust Stripe had earned by being excellent, responsive, and deeply aligned with the needs of its audience.

Even its branding choices reflected this. Quiet typography. Simple product pages. A sense of restraint that said: *This is for serious people doing serious work.* Stripe didn't shout. It didn't need to. The community spoke for it.

And when people did gather, in forums, on Twitter, in founder circles, there was a shared understanding. A feeling that choosing Stripe meant choosing a set of values: clarity, rigor, momentum, belief in builders.

That's what made the community powerful. Not its size. Not even its engagement. But it's **coherence**.

Stripe reminds us that community-led strategy isn't always loud. Sometimes it's quiet excellence, repeated consistently. Sometimes it's infrastructure, product, tone, or trust.

Sometimes, the most powerful community is the one that forms because you've done your job so well; people want to talk about it together.

Case Study 6: LEGO Ideas – Let the Fans Design the Future

For decades, LEGO was seen as a toy company. A brilliant one, yes, but its product decisions came from within. Designers sketched, engineers refined, marketers planned. Customers were customers.

Then something shifted.

The internet made fan culture more visible and more participatory. Adult fans began showcasing custom LEGO builds online. Communities formed. People weren't just building sets. They were building **worlds**.

LEGO could've ignored this or tried to control it. But instead, they leaned in, not with lip service, but with structure.

They launched **LEGO Ideas**, a platform that lets anyone submit their set design. If a submission got 10,000 votes from the community, LEGO would review it. If it passed the review, they'd manufacture and sell it, crediting the designer, paying royalties, and publicly celebrating the win.

This wasn't a marketing stunt. It was a **strategic shift**: from product-first to **community-powered innovation**.

Suddenly, the line between fan and designer disappeared. A schoolteacher in Japan could have their submarine model turned into a global product. A sci-fi enthusiast in Poland could design a tribute set for a classic film. The company became a canvas, and fans became part of the creative process.

What made LEGO Ideas work wasn't just the vote threshold. It was the **clarity and care** around participation. Guidelines were simple. Submissions were visible. Feedback was respectful. And most importantly, wins were celebrated, not just by LEGO, but by the entire community.

This created a virtuous loop: Enthusiasm sparked creativity → creativity drew in more fans → the best ideas became real → reality fueled trust → trust fueled more participation.

Importantly, LEGO didn't treat this as a separate initiative. Over time, the company wove fan-created sets into its core product lines. They saw the community not just as inspiration, but as a **strategic partner**, one that could sense cultural trends, test demand, and surface fresh thinking long before internal teams could.

LEGO Ideas proves that innovation doesn't always require R&D labs or internal brainstorms. Sometimes, it requires listening. Sometimes, it requires **letting go of the monopoly on genius** and building the systems that allow brilliance to come in from the outside.

Most of all, it requires humility: the willingness to say, We don't have all the answers. But maybe someone out there does.

And when a brand does that well, the community doesn't just contribute. It starts to feel like it **owns part of the future**.

Case Study 7: Stack Overflow – Reputation, Rigor, and Clarity

Stack Overflow isn't warm. It doesn't welcome you with memes or onboarding rituals. There are no friendly group chats, no emoji-laced introductions. And yet, it remains one of the most impactful communities in the world of software development.

Why? Because it answers a particular question, with near-religious discipline: How do we solve technical problems, precisely and publicly, so others don't have to ask them again?

The result is a community optimized not for conversation, but for **knowledge curation, not** for expression, but for **clarity**. You're not there to talk, you're there to answer. Or be answered. Or find a solution that's already been validated by others like you.

That model, while narrow, has built an extraordinary **public resource**. Tens of millions of developers turn to Stack Overflow every month. The most valuable answers are visible at a glance. Search engines point there first. The community's contribution has shaped how programming is learned globally.

But what makes Stack Overflow work isn't the software. It's the **structure**.

From the start, the platform was designed for accountability. Answers could be upvoted or downvoted. Reputation points were earned, not given. Privileges were unlocked over time. Moderation wasn't top-down; it was built into the architecture, based on a logic of **earned trust**.

This created a deeply meritocratic culture, but also, at times, an intimidating one.

Newcomers often found the environment harsh. Mistakes were corrected bluntly. Poorly worded questions were flagged, closed, and sometimes ridiculed. And while this enforced a kind of quality control, it also created a **barrier to belonging**.

Stack Overflow learned from this. Over time, it introduced tone guidelines. Expanded mentorship tools. Softened some interactions without sacrificing rigor. But the tension remains: how do you maintain high standards while also inviting people to grow?

What Stack Overflow demonstrates, uniquely, is the power of **communal editing**. This is not a place of constant conversation. It's a **living document**, collectively refined. A place where your contribution may live for years, helping thousands, even if no one ever replies to thank you.

It's also a place where identity is built through **consistency, not personality**. No bios. No status games. Just you, your answers, and the quiet recognition of doing hard things well.

If there's a lesson here, it's this: not all communities need to feel social. Some need to feel **useful**. And when structure is aligned with purpose, when the design reinforces the values you care about, you can build something that lasts longer than any one member. Something that becomes part of the **internet's infrastructure**.

Case Study 8: Airbnb – Trust as Infrastructure

Airbnb doesn't look like a community at first glance. It's a marketplace. A platform. A tech company that connects people who have homes with people who need a place to stay.

But beneath the transactions lies a subtler truth: Airbnb scaled because it built **systems of trust** between strangers, across cultures, in cities around the world. And trust, as it turns out, is the community's most precious resource.

In the early days, that trust was fragile. The idea of sleeping in a stranger's house, or hosting one, felt risky, awkward, even absurd. What turned it from a fringe concept to a mainstream habit wasn't just marketing. It was **designing trust into every layer** of the experience.

Airbnb introduced profiles, reviews, and ratings, not as afterthoughts, but as **core architecture**. Guests saw who they were staying with. Hosts saw who was coming. Both sides had a voice. This mutual visibility didn't just reduce fraud; it created **relational awareness**, which softened risk.

The company also used storytelling strategically. From early on, it featured the real stories of hosts and guests. Not polished testimonials, but small human moments: a homemade breakfast, a family reunion, a musician on tour. This wasn't just branding. It was a **community narrative**, an invitation for others to see themselves as part of something bigger.

As Airbnb grew, so did its need for community infrastructure. Local host clubs emerged, with some supported by Airbnb and others forming organically. Hosts shared tips, troubles, and tricks of the trade. Cities became learning environments. The product team began to listen.

Airbnb didn't just allow these groups to form. It recognized their strategic value. Hosts weren't just suppliers, they were **ambassadors**, shaping guest experiences, local economies, and brand perception on the ground. Eventually, Airbnb formalized its support: meetups, content libraries, and host mentorship programs. But the culture of **peer connection and shared stewardship** had already taken hold.

Of course, community at scale is never simple. Regulatory battles, safety incidents, and public scrutiny introduced new complexities. But at its core, Airbnb has always returned to the same insight: people don't just want a place to stay. They want to **feel safe in someone else's space**. And that feeling can't be faked.

What Airbnb teaches is that community doesn't always look like conversation. Sometimes, it seems like **consistency**. Like a review that makes you feel safe. A message that makes you feel seen. A check-in that feels human, not transactional.

It reminds us that strategy is often invisible. But when it's rooted in trust, it becomes **everywhere at once**.

Case Study 9: Peloton – Motivation in Motion

Peloton didn't invent at-home fitness. It reinvented the **emotional context** of working out alone.

Before Peloton, home fitness was often solitary. A DVD. A treadmill in the garage. A silent subscription app. What Peloton did was inject presence, *live instructors, real-time stats, and a leaderboard* into an otherwise isolated space. Suddenly, you weren't just riding a bike. You were riding **with** people and being seen doing it.

That visibility changed everything.

From the beginning, Peloton understood that community isn't just about social features. It's about **shared rhythm**. When you show up to the same class, at the same time, with familiar faces and familiar voices, a kind of soft bond begins to form. You start to recognize usernames. You hear your name shouted out mid-ride. You become part of the tempo.

Peloton's instructors amplified this tenfold. They weren't just trainers, they were **hosts**, coaches, even cultural figures. Their presence became central to the brand, not peripheral. They created emotional continuity between classes, seasons, and goals. And they did it in direct address: *You've got this. You're not alone. Keep going.*

In doing so, they helped members do what few fitness brands achieve: **tie identity to commitment**. A Peloton user wasn't just exercising. They were becoming someone who shows up. Someone in the community. Someone on a journey.

Peloton layered this identity work with innovative structures. Leaderboards. Badges. Hashtags that let you declare your micro-affiliation, #BlackGirlMagic, #StayHomeStayMotivated, and #

MomsOfPeloton. These weren't marketing tags. They were **cultural signals**, soft containers of belonging within the larger ecosystem.

And perhaps most importantly, Peloton gave people **a reason to return**. Not through pressure, but through programming. Weekly rides. Seasonal challenges. Birthday shoutouts. Community milestones. These were not gimmicks. They were **rituals**, ways to make time feel structured and progress feel witnessed.

Of course, community at scale has its trade-offs. As Peloton grew, the intimacy of early engagement changed. New competitors emerged. The pandemic's tailwinds faded. But through it all, Peloton's core lesson remained:

People don't stay for the product. They stay for the feeling of **moving together**, even apart.

Peloton's story reminds us that community doesn't need a forum. It doesn't require conversation. It needs **continuity, shared effort, and emotional anchoring**. And when those three things are present, even a solo ride in your basement can feel like a gathering.

Case Study 10: Y Combinator – Cohorts and Credibility

Y Combinator isn't just an accelerator. It's a **rite of passage**. From the outside, YC is about funding startups: a short program, a bit of equity, and access to investors. But anyone who's been inside knows it's something else entirely, a community that **redefines what it means to be a founder**, and who gets to belong.

The structure is deceptively simple. Startups apply. A handful are accepted. Those selected enter a tightly run cohort, participate in group dinners, meet partners, share progress, and, at the end, present to an audience of investors on Demo Day. But the real value lies in the spaces between those events.

Founders aren't just given capital. They're given **context**. They learn how other founders think, where they struggle, and how they communicate with clarity under pressure. They sit side by side, week by week, building trust through shared pace. They're taught not just how to pitch, but how to **believe** in themselves, in their teammates, in the market they're shaping.

YC's genius lies in two moves.

First, it **engineered belonging through selectivity**. Getting in wasn't easy, and that friction created gravity. Acceptance wasn't just a door to funding. It was a signal, a badge, a story to carry. And once inside, that shared achievement created a fast track to mutual respect. Everyone knew what it had taken to get there.

Second, it is designed for **peer accountability, not top-down hierarchy**. Partners offer guidance, but the authentic culture lives in the cohort. Founders push each other, help debug each other's pitches, and share wins and failures with raw honesty. There's no competition for attention. The attention is collective, and the success of one startup becomes *fuel* for others.

That dynamic doesn't end after the program. YC's alum network, now thousands strong, is one of the most quietly influential support systems in tech, with advice threads. Warm intros. Emotional debriefs. A place where, years after Demo Day, founders still return when they hit walls they can't climb alone.

The result is a community where reputation compounds over time, not because of marketing, but because of **relationships, results, and remembered effort**.

YC's model doesn't scale easily, but it doesn't try to. Its strength is in **intensity, not volume**. It knows that depth of connection builds long-term value. And that the best communities aren't the ones that grow rapidly. They're the ones that stay true, over time.

What YC proves is this: When you gather people around a shared ambition, with clear stakes, honest feedback, and meaningful thresholds, you don't just accelerate companies. You **forge a generation of builders who never forget where they began**.

Case Study 11: Reddit – Chaos, Culture, and Subcommunity

Reddit didn't begin as a community. It started as a canvas.

The earliest version was a bare-bones link aggregator, a place to post, vote, and comment. But almost immediately, something strange happened: users began organizing around **interest, not identity**. They created subreddits. They built their own cultures. And Reddit let them.

That choice, **to decentralize from the start**, defined everything that followed.

Today, Reddit is less a singular community than a **collection of thousands**, each with its tone, language, rules, and rituals. From r/AskHistorians to r/WallStreetBets, r/MadeMeSmile to r/AmItheAsshole, the platform hosts humor, expertise, conflict, support, and absurdity, often all at once.

The magic isn't in any one subreddit. It's in the **system of permission and autonomy** that allows each space to be wildly itself.

Moderators are not company employees. They are volunteers, often fiercely protective of their community's norms. They set rules, enforce tone, and ban bad actors. They are, in many ways, the **unsung infrastructure of Reddit's resilience**.

This model isn't without friction. It can lead to inconsistency, controversy, and chaos. But it also produces **intensity**. When people are allowed to shape their own space, they care about it more. When they care, they contribute. When they contribute, culture forms. And culture is what keeps people coming back.

Reddit has leaned into this. Rather than trying to unify the platform under one aesthetic or set of values, it has embraced

pluralism. Product updates focus on mod tools, voting mechanics, and community safety. The company intervenes sparingly, only when legal or ethical boundaries are crossed.

And yet, out of this decentralized sprawl, Reddit has surfaced **some of the most relevant and durable internet cultures** of the last decade. Movements have begun there. Memes have gone global. Financial markets have been jolted by forum chatter. AMA (Ask Me Anything) formats have become part of the mainstream.

All this without flashy branding. Without hero narratives. Just **structure, freedom, and time**.

If Reddit teaches us anything, it's that you don't always need to curate the message. Sometimes, you need to **create the conditions for expression**, and let culture do what it does best: surprise you.

Reddit didn't manufacture community. It trusted people to build their own and stayed out of the way just enough.

Case Study 12: Khan Academy – Mission at the Center

Khan Academy began with a simple gesture: Sal Khan tutoring his cousin in math over YouTube.

What started as a helpful video grew into a library. That library grew into a platform. And that platform became one of the most trusted names in online education, used by tens of millions, from students in rural villages to classrooms in significant cities.

But content alone didn't build that trust. **The community did so** quietly, in layers.

Khan Academy's power lies in its unwavering clarity of purpose: to offer a free, world-class education for anyone, anywhere. That clarity created not just consistency, but also **alignment**. People showed up not just to consume, but to contribute because they believed in the mission.

Some contributed time, translating content, subtitling lessons, and adapting explanations for local contexts. Others shared knowledge, educators and volunteers answered questions, supported struggling learners, and built public discussion threads. And some contributed code, developers enhancing the platform, reporting bugs, shaping features for greater accessibility.

None of this was top-down. Khan Academy didn't recruit ambassadors with branded gear or leaderboard points. Instead, it created **lightweight paths for contribution**: forums, feedback forms, open-source documentation, and clear guidelines. It trusted people to show up with good intent and supported them when they did.

Over time, a culture emerged. A culture of *helping quietly*. A culture where questions are met with encouragement, not shame.

Where mistakes aren't punished but explored, where learners of all ages feel not just tolerated, but *welcomed*, whether they're 9 or 90, in school or learning for the first time.

What makes Khan Academy's community work isn't social virality or brand hype. It's **emotional safety paired with intellectual generosity**. Students trust the space. Parents trust the content. Educators trust the tone. And volunteers trust the process.

That trust became the foundation for resilience. When the COVID-19 pandemic closed schools worldwide, Khan Academy saw usage skyrocket. But its infrastructure held, not just technically, but socially. Why? Because the community already knew how to support one another. The scaffolding was there. The care was in place.

Khan Academy proves that community in education doesn't always need fanfare. It needs **mission, trust, and the humility to let learners lead**.

And in that kind of space, even a quiet act, a translated video, a patient reply, can ripple outward. Not as engagement. But as a **transformation**.

Appendix C: Tools & Platforms

Infrastructure for Belonging

Every community builder, sooner or later, faces the same question: *What tool should we use?*

It seems like a technical question: Slack or Discord? Circle or Mighty Networks? A custom stack or an off-the-shelf app? But beneath that question is something more human: *What kind of space are we trying to build? And how do we want people to feel inside it?*

Because tools aren't neutral, they shape behavior. They set norms. They whisper instructions to their users, even when no one is watching.

A real-time chat tool encourages speed. A forum slows things down. A voice room introduces vulnerability. A leaderboard amplifies performance. A comment thread can either encourage or flatten hierarchy. A tool with a strong permissioning signal structure. One without it creates ambiguity.

So, the question isn't just, What tool do we need? It's what kind of culture do we want to support, and what tools best reinforce that culture over time?

There's no perfect platform. There's only one **fit**.

Some communities thrive in frictionless spaces, characterized by simplicity, minimalism, and low maintenance. Others require layers: onboarding flows, role-based access, event integrations, and reporting dashboards. Some communities are event-driven; others are content-driven; others grow from intimate conversation. The tooling must meet the **tempo, texture, and tone** of the experience you want to create.

It's also a question of **ownership and access**. Who controls the data? Who can moderate? Who can scale the space as needs evolve? Will this tool grow with you, or limit your next strategic move? If the platform disappears, what do you lose, and what can you carry forward?

Community-led strategy means making intentional trade-offs, not just going where everyone else is. Sometimes that means choosing a less popular tool because it better matches your values. Sometimes it means integrating several tools to bridge gaps. And sometimes it means building something custom, because nothing else quite holds what you're trying to create.

But whatever you choose, the point is not to chase features. It's to support **connection**.

And when your tools disappear into the background, when members don't think about the interface, but feel the belonging, that's when you know your infrastructure is working.

In the next section, we'll explore the community tech stack in three layers: **Core Platforms**, **Engagement Layers**, and **Operational Tools**, each aligned with different phases and philosophies of community development.

Core Platforms – Where Belonging Lives

Every community needs a home. Not just a landing page, but a place where people **return**.

Core platforms are where that happens. They hold the rhythms, relationships, and rituals that give a community its shape. They are the vessels for belonging, and they quietly shape what kind of belonging is possible.

Choosing a core platform means deciding where your members will show up, how they'll communicate, and what norms will form through repetition. It's not a matter of brand aesthetics. It's a matter of **behavioral design**.

Take Slack, for instance. Built for teams, it's fast, real-time, channel-driven. It creates immediacy, but also impermanence. Messages flow quickly. If you miss a day, you might miss a thread. Great for high-context, high-trust groups. Tough for asynchronous depth.

Discord evolved from gaming culture, voice rooms, text channels, roles, bots, and a looser structure. It feels like a living room with layers: public spaces, private corners, side conversations humming beneath the surface. Rich in culture. Complex in governance.

Circle and Mighty Networks, by contrast, are designed *for* communities. They combine forum-like permanence with social media familiarity. Discussions are threaded. Content can be organized. Events and courses can be embedded. They offer scaffolding, but also opinions about how a community should flow.

Facebook Groups remain ubiquitous, especially for casual or mass-market communities. Easy to start, but hard to truly own. You rent the space, but Facebook owns the house. And what the algorithm giveth, it can also take away.

Then there are custom platforms, built in-house, often by companies with specific needs or a strong product-first identity. This path allows for total control: design, data, and user experience. But it comes with a cost. Maintenance. Complexity.

The need to become a *platform company*, not just a community host.

No matter what you choose, the key is to understand your community's **needs and tendencies**. Do they value synchronicity or depth? Do they want ambient presence, or clear boundaries? Will they check in daily, or drop by when needed? Will they post freely, or need gentle prompts?

And perhaps most importantly: will the platform you choose **invite them into a shared rhythm**?

That's what a core platform does well. It creates predictability, context, and room to show up as yourself, or become more of who you're trying to be.

In the next section, we'll explore **Engagement Layers**, the supporting tools that enhance your core space with programming, connection, recognition, and more.

Engagement Layers – Designing for Momentum

If the core platform is the home, then engagement layers are the **furniture, music, and rituals** that make people want to stay.

They help shape the day-to-day experience of being in community: how people connect, how they participate, how they're recognized, and how they build trust. These tools are about **designing momentum**, the feeling that something is constantly unfolding, and that you matter to it.

Start with events. Platforms like Zoom, Butter, Luma, and Hopin create structured moments of live presence, gatherings that punctuate the asynchronous rhythm of the platform. A well-timed event isn't just content. It's **coordination**. It's shared time. It reminds members they're not alone, even if they spend most of their time watching from the edges.

Then there are matchmaking tools: Intros, Orbit, Donut (for Slack), and custom Airtable setups. These create lightweight serendipity, randomized pairings, curated intros, and micro-cohorts. They introduce movement into the static. The "oh, I didn't know you were here too" moment that expands the map of belonging.

Content layers matter too. Newsletters. Recaps. Highlight reels. Tools like Mailchimp, Substack, or native email integrations help community builders narrate what's happening. Because community isn't just about events, it's about **sense-making**. When you help people see what they're part of, they show up with more intention.

Recognition tools also play a quiet but vital role. Whether it's badges (via Commsor or Orbit), points, shoutouts, or public rituals like "Member of the Month," these tools **surface contribution**. They answer the question: *Does anyone see what I'm doing here?* The answer doesn't need to be loud. But it needs to be clear.

And then there's automation, tools like Zapier, Make (formerly Integromat), or native workflows. These reduce the manual load of management and allow for thoughtful touchpoints at scale. A welcome message after sign-up. A follow-up two weeks later. A personalized nudge after a big event. Automation done well doesn't feel robotic; it feels **responsive**.

Together, these layers create **texture**. They make the space feel alive, curated, and intentional, without overwhelming or overengineering it. The goal isn't more tools. It's the **right layer at the right time**, in service of connection.

Next, we'll turn to the third tier of your stack: **Operational Tools**, the behind-the-scenes infrastructure that keeps everything coherent, measurable, and responsive as your community scales.

Operational Tools – Building for Resilience

Behind every thriving community is a messy spreadsheet. Or five. Maybe ten. Because community building isn't just emotional labor, it's **operational labor**. It involves scheduling, tagging, analyzing, responding, prioritizing, and remembering. And while most members will never see this layer, it's what makes the visible experience feel seamless.

Operational tools are the systems that help you track what matters, streamline what's repetitive, and protect what's sacred.

Start with analytics. Tools like Orbit, Common Room, and Talkbase help make sense of who's contributing, how often, and where. They connect the dots between activity and impact, surfacing your most engaged members, tracking onboarding drop-off, and even connecting community engagement to business outcomes like product feedback or retention.

But metrics without meaning are dangerous. The point isn't to chase charts. It's to **find signals that reflect your values**. Contribution over clicks. Belonging to bounce rates. Activation over acquisition. Data can guide, but only when rooted in context.

Then there's member management. As your space grows, you'll need to know: Who's here? What role do they play? What journey are they on? CRMs like Airtable, Notion, or bespoke tools can help track relationships, not as transactions, but as **evolving stories**. This allows you to reach out thoughtfully, design better programming, and remember who's quietly shaping the space.

Documentation tools matter more than you think. Notion, Coda, and Google Docs become your **community memory**, a living record of how things work, what's happened, and what's next. This clarity protects against drift. It creates onboarding paths not just for members, but for future moderators, collaborators, and co-stewards.

And then there's team coordination. As soon as you have more than one person supporting a community, internal tools like Slack, Asana, Trello, or Linear become vital. They allow you to move faster without losing alignment. Community work is often reactive, but the best teams make space for a **proactive rhythm**: planning, checking in, reflecting as a habit.

Finally, there's tooling for safety and governance. Moderation tools. Reporting systems. Escalation flows. These aren't glamorous, but they're essential. A space can only feel open if it's also **protected**. And operational clarity is what allows that protection to feel calm, not punitive.

When used with intention, operational tools don't just increase efficiency. They extend **care**.

They allow you to hold complexity without confusion. To grow without losing soul. To stay grounded in purpose, even when things move fast.

In the end, your tools won't build your community for you. But they'll help you hold the space **with more clarity, trust, and capacity**.

Tools as Strategic Signals

By now, it's clear: tools are not just utilities. They are **strategic signals**, quiet reflections of your values, your structure, your ambitions, and your care.

Choosing a community tool isn't just about features. It's about **inviting a kind of behavior**. Do you want fast back-and-forth or thoughtful pacing? Do you want content to be permanent or ephemeral? Do you want hierarchy, or porous edges? Every platform nudges people in a direction.

But more than that, tooling choices say something about **what kind of relationship you're building**.

A community built on Discord feels different than one built on Circle. A space that uses weekly live events feels different than one built around deep written discussion. A group that tags contributors, rewards rituals, and archives learnings sends a different message than one that resets every Monday.

And that's the point. Your stack is your **architecture of culture**.

There is no perfect combination. But there is a coherent one. A setup that reflects your tone. That supports your members' needs. That reduces your manual load while deepening the connection.

The best stacks are modular. Evolving. Honest. And the best community builders aren't obsessed with tools. They're obsessed with **fit, flow, and feeling**.

Because when your tools disappear into the background, what emerges is the thing that truly matters: **belonging you can feel, but never quite measure.**

Appendix D: Glossary of Terms

A Living Language of Community-Led Thinking

Language is infrastructure. It shapes how we think, what we notice, and how we relate to one another.

Throughout this book, we've used terms that come from product strategy, systems thinking, sociology, and cultural work. What follows is not a dry index, but a **living glossary**, a way to hold shared meaning as the conversation around community-led strategy continues to evolve.

Activation

The moment when a member takes a meaningful first action, such as posting, contributing, or attending. It's the shift from passive observer to **engaged participant**.

Ambassador

A community member who embodies the culture, supports others, and often extends the space's reach. Ambassadors are not influencers; they are **relational leaders**.

Audience

People who are paying attention. They may be loyal. They may be engaged. But the relationship is **primarily directional**; you speak, they listen. A community listens back.

Cohort

A group of people who join at the same time, experience the same flow, and often build stronger ties through **synchronous progression**. Cohorts add structure and pace to community onboarding.

Community

Not just a group of users. A network of people with shared context, care, and contribution, who derive meaning from being part of something together. Communities form when people see each other, not just the brand.

Community Health

A holistic view of the ecosystem's integrity. Not just engagement stats, but emotional climate, member retention, trust, diversity of participation, and conflict resilience.

Community-Led

A strategic posture where community is not a support function or marketing layer, but a **core driver** of business value, through feedback, innovation, culture, growth, and more.

Community-Led Growth

Growth powered by the community itself, through referrals, word-of-mouth, content creation, events, or evangelism. Not just unpaid marketing, but **participatory expansion**.

Community Stack

The integrated set of tools, core platforms, engagement layers, and operational infrastructure that support the ecosystem. Your stack isn't just tech; it's **strategy made visible**.

Contribution

Any act that shapes the space. It can be visible (like starting a thread) or subtle (welcoming a newcomer). Healthy communities are defined by **many forms of contribution**, not just the loudest voices.

Contribution Threshold

The level of comfort, confidence, or context required for a member to move from lurking to posting. Lowering this threshold, through design, tone, and trust, is key to activation.

Defensibility

How difficult it is for others to replicate your community's value. In the business context, defensibility often comes from **shared history, emotional resonance, and organic loyalty**, not just features or content.

Engagement

Not just clicks or comments. Authentic engagement is **participation with intention**, a sign that someone feels agency, relevance, and belonging inside the space.

Exit to Community

A model of long-term sustainability where the ownership, governance, or direction of a community is transitioned, fully or partially, to its members. A radical inversion of top-down strategy, rooted in **shared stewardship**.

Flywheel

A self-reinforcing loop of value. In communities, this might look like: contribution leads to recognition, which leads to retention, which encourages more contribution. The **community flywheel** gets stronger the more it turns.

Governance

The structures, formal or informal, that define who holds power, how decisions get made, and what accountability looks like inside a community. Governance, when done well, is **quietly felt but rarely resented**.

Lurker

A participant who observes without posting. Often misunderstood as disengaged, lurkers may actually be learning, absorbing, or simply not ready. Communities thrive when **lurking is respected, not shamed**.

Moderation

The practice of guiding a space toward its intended culture. Not just about removing bad behavior, but **shaping tone**, **holding boundaries**, and **honoring norms**.

Network Effect

A dynamic where each new member adds value to all others. In a community, this often depends on **interaction quality**, not just quantity; one thoughtful member may do more for network strength than 50 silent signups.

Onboarding

The process of welcoming and orienting new members. More than logistics, onboarding is a **cultural invitation**, helping people know not just what to do, but how to feel.

Psychological Safety

The sense that one can speak, ask, risk, and show up without fear of ridicule or harm. It is the **precondition for trust** and the soil in which the community grows.

Ritual

A recurring moment or pattern that gives shape to the experience of belonging. Rituals are not just repeated actions; they are **carriers of meaning**.

Scaling Soul

The art of growing a community's reach or complexity without losing its **core identity, tone, and trust**. One of the most complex challenges in community-led strategy is the need to balance multiple objectives.

Signal

A behavior, action, or pattern that offers meaningful insight into a member's mindset or the health of a community. Signals are different from metrics; they require **interpretation, not just measurement**.

Touchpoint

Any moment of contact, automated, personal, synchronous, or ambient, where a member encounters the community's tone and intention. Touchpoints are the **breadcrumbs of belonging**.

Closing: From Reading to Rebuilding

If you've made it here, you already understand something that can't be taught in slides or spreadsheets:

Community isn't a feature. It's a force.

> ➤ A force that rewires the way we think about value.
> ➤ A force that reshapes how products grow, how cultures form, and how trust is earned.
> ➤ A force that reminds us, especially in this era of automation, velocity, and digital noise, that people still want to belong to something

This book has offered you frameworks. Language. Mental models. Case studies. But strategy alone is not the work. The work involves paying attention and listening, even when it's inconvenient—trusting people with small bits of ownership. Choosing generosity over scale, and clarity over noise.

The work is invisible before it's undeniable.

You won't always be able to measure it. The most potent moments might not show up in dashboards. You'll wonder if it's working. You'll hit plateaus. You'll watch things grow sideways, or too fast, or too quiet. You'll have to decide whether to push, pause, or hold the door open longer. But if you stay close to the people, their needs, their context, their rhythms, you'll find your way. And when it works, you won't be the hero of the story. The people will be.

That's the paradox of community-led strategy: the more power you give away, the more resilient the system becomes. Not because it runs itself. But because it **belongs to more than just you**.

So, build with care. Build slowly if you must. But make **like it matters**.

Because it does.

And we'll need more spaces, urgently, generously, wisely, where people don't just transact, but **transform together**.

About the Author

Sabir Chatte is a strategist, advisor, and cultural systems thinker with over 25 years of experience helping organizations design for belonging, not just efficiency. He has worked with early-stage startups, global nonprofits, and Fortune 100 companies to shape community ecosystems that fuel product feedback, retention, innovation, and trust.

His work blends insights from sociology, product development, and narrative design, anchored in the belief that the future belongs to organizations that are not just networked, but *nourishing*.

He lives between Lisbon and Singapore, spending most of his time listening to communities that are inventing new ways of working, governing, and growing.

About the Publisher

Welcome to The Book On Publishing

At The Book On Publishing, we believe in rewriting the rules of learning. Whether you're chasing your next big idea, building a better life, or simply curious about what should have been taught in school, you've come to the right place.

We're a platform built for dreamers, doers, and lifelong learners, offering bold, practical books and tools that empower you to take charge of your journey. From real-world skills to mindset mastery, we publish the book on what matters.

No fluff. No lectures. Just what you need to know, delivered with clarity, purpose, and a spark of curiosity.

Start exploring. Start growing. Start writing your story.

Read more at https://thebookon.ca.

Acknowledgment of AI Assistance

Portions of this book were developed with the support of ChatGPT, an AI language model created by OpenAI. While every word has been carefully reviewed and refined by the author, ChatGPT served as a valuable tool for brainstorming, editing, and structuring ideas. Its assistance helped accelerate the creative process and bring clarity to complex topics.